WARSAW 1920

By the same author

Chopin: A Biography
The Battle for the Marchlands
Paderewski
The Polish Way
The Last King of Poland
The Forgotten Few
Holy Madness: Romantics, Patriots and Revolutionaries, 1776–1871
1812: Napoleon's Fatal March on Moscow
Rites of Peace: The Fall of Napoleon and the Congress of Vienna

WARSAW 1920

Lenin's Failed Conquest of Europe

———◆———

ADAM ZAMOYSKI

Harper
Press

HarperCollins*Publishers*
77–85 Fulham Palace Road,
Hammersmith, London W6 8JB
www.harpercollins.co.uk

Published by HarperCollins*Publishers* 2008

1

The author asserts the moral right to be
identified as the author of this work

A catalogue record for this book is
available from the British Library

ISBN 978-0-00-722552-1

Set in Minion by Thomson Digital

Printed and bound in Great Britain by Clays Ltd, St Ives plc

Mixed Sources
Product group from well-managed
forests and other controlled sources
www.fsc.org Cert no. SW-COC-1806
© 1996 Forest Stewardship Council
FSC

FSC is a non-profit international organisation established to promote the
responsible management of the world's forests. Products carrying the FSC
label are independently certified to assure consumers that they come
from forests that are managed to meet the social, economic and
ecological needs of present and future generations.

Find out more about HarperCollins and the environment at
www.harpercollins.co.uk/green

CONTENTS

ILLUSTRATIONS

Piłsudski reviewing volunteers setting off for the front. *(Centralne Archiwum Wojskowe, Warsaw)*

Kamenev with soldiers of the Red Army. *(The David King Archive, London)*

Russian infantry on parade. *(The David King Archive, London)*

Russian heavy artillery outside Warsaw, August 1920. *(The David King Archive, London)*

A colour party of Red cavalry, spring 1920. *(The David King Archive, London)*

The Red cavalry's secret weapon, the *tachanka*. *(The David King Archive, London)*

Polish field artillery in Pińsk, spring 1920. *(Centralne Archiwum Wojskowe, Warsaw)*

The Polish 16th Lancers marching through Równe, March 1920. *(Biblioteka Książąt Czartoryskich, Kraków)*

Polish heavy artillery in Ukraine, May 1920. *(Centralne Archiwum Wojskowe, Warsaw)*

The Polish Air Force's Kościuszko Squadron, made up of American volunteers. *(The Polish Institute and Sikorski Museum, London)*

Polish armoured train. *(Centralne Archiwum Wojskowe, Warsaw)*

A Russian divisional radio transmitter. *(The David King Archive, London)*

Żeligowski. *(Centralne Archiwum Wojskowe, Warsaw)*

MAPS

INTRODUCTION

It may come as something of a surprise to most people that a battle as decisive as Marathon or Waterloo took place in Europe between the end of the First World War in 1918 and the outbreak of the Second in 1939. Dramatic and fateful as they were, the events that took place at the gates of Warsaw in August 1920 have sunk into oblivion.

This is the more surprising as they had a profound effect on the politics of the 1920s and 1930s, on the course of the Second World War, and on the peace settlement of 1945, as well as a lasting one on attitudes throughout Europe – figures such as Stalin, Churchill and De Gaulle were personally involved, while others such as Mussolini, Franco and Hitler took careful note.

The reasons for this eclipse are not hard to find. One is that while the battle did indeed alter the course of history, it did so by preventing something from taking place rather than by reversing it; this meant that it had no palpable impact on anyone not directly involved. Another is that historians of the time were mostly preoccupied with other themes, such as composing triumphalist accounts of the Great War from their own national standpoint. If they mentioned the battle of Warsaw at all, they tended to follow the lead of Soviet historians, who, not wishing to accept that their country had lost a war, treated it as part of the Russian Civil War, which the Soviets had won. Finally, the Second World War reversed the effect of the 1920 contest, seemingly rendering it irrelevant in the greater scheme of things. A negative view of Eastern Europe and the wholesale acceptance of socialist orthodoxies by Western historians in the decades following it did the rest.

This little book does not pretend to fill the resulting void. All it can aspire to is to provide an outline of the events, and specialists will find my generalisations wanting. Since the political and diplomatic background has been extensively covered by others (see Further Reading, page 149), I have concentrated on the military operations, and in particular on providing a synthesis accessible to the general reader and a succinct overview of what happened and how. This necessarily excludes dozens of minor actions and ignores the part played by many lesser actors, some of them of crucial importance. Nor can it give anything but a hint of the horrors and the heroism involved, or of the sense, which comes through all personal accounts and contemporary documents, that this was a crisis of European civilization.

I was fortunate enough to take an interest in these events some years ago, when many participants and even a few key players were still alive. There was something both exciting and unreal about sitting in a seedy London flat or a clapboard house somewhere in the great expanses of American suburbia, talking to someone who had stared death in the face at the end of a lance or seen the glint of Trotsky's spectacles. It was also deeply rewarding, as it helped me to bridge the gulf between how events appear from documents and how they are experienced on the ground. Sadly, it was not then possible to talk to participants on the Soviet side, which would have added a remarkable perspective.

In spite, or perhaps because, of its contentious nature, the Polish–Soviet conflict of 1919–21 is extremely well covered in Polish and Russian, and there has never been any shortage of written sources. All of the essential operational documents were accessible, either in print or in archives, remarkably early on, and little has emerged in the past two decades to shed the kind of new light that would prompt a reinterpretation of the events. And although the numerous studies produced in Poland and Russia between the wars are rarely free of bias, they do contain a wealth of solid information. Perhaps surprisingly in the circumstances, it is the even more numerous accounts and studies by participants that provide some of the most interesting material. Although they tend to be written from a partisan and often blinkered position, an intelligent reading that takes this into account can yield rich pickings.

As the participants and witnesses I was able to interview are no longer with us, I would like in the first place to thank them, and particularly the late Aleksander Pragłowski, Kornel Krzeczunowicz, Władysław Anders and Adam Minkiewicz. I am also indebted to Stanisław Biegański of the Józef Piłsudski Institute and Wacław Milewski of the Sikorski Institute in London; to Bogusław Winid, to Dr Andrzej Czesław Żak of the Central Army Archive and Dr Grzegorz Nowik of the Army Centre for Historical Studies in Warsaw, to Professor Andrzej Nowak, Bogdan Gancarz, and to my friend Norman Davies. As always, Shervie Price anticipated the queries of the standard reader.

Adam Zamoyski
London
September 2007

Europe after the Paris peace settlement

1

Old Scores and New Dawns

ON 28 JUNE 1919, a multitude of frock-coated statesmen gathered in the great hall of mirrors of the palace of Versailles for the ceremonial signature of a treaty between Great Britain, France, the United States and their allies on the one hand, and a defeated Germany on the other. The document fixed not only the borders of Germany and the reparations to be paid by her; it redrew the political map of Central Europe. It separated Germany from Russia by resurrecting Poland and bringing into being a number of new states, from Estonia in the north to the Czecho-Slovak Republic in the south. This was done partly in the new spirit of national self-determination advocated by the US President Woodrow Wilson, and also to create buffers against any future attempts at German expansion. This new order would, it was hoped, draw a line under the militaristic imperialism of the nineteenth century and guarantee a lasting peace.

This peace had cost millions of lives and irretrievable resources. It had robbed countries such as Britain and France of a generation of young men. The price paid had shaken the faith of society in the institutions that had led to the war, creating an ideological crisis whose profound social and political effects could be felt at every level. Yet within a year of its signature, the peace and the political settlement the treaty had brought into being were threatened with annihilation.

In the summer of 1920 a seemingly unstoppable Russian army was sweeping across Poland with the avowed aim of bringing about revolution in Germany and using that country as a springboard for imposing Bolshevik-style governments on the other nations of Europe. 'By attacking Poland we are attacking the Allies,' warned the leader of the Bolshevik government in Russia, Vladimir Illich Lenin; 'by destroying the Polish army we are destroying the Versailles peace, upon which rests the whole present system of international relations.'[1]

Exhausted by the blood-letting of the Great War, ravaged by the influenza epidemic sweeping the world and wary of the mass of unemployed soldiers resentful of a system that could not provide them with a dignified future, neither the United States, which was rapidly slipping back into isolationism, nor the Entente, as Great Britain and France were commonly referred to, was in a position to defend its cherished peace settlement. All they could do was look on anxiously as the fate of Europe, and by extension that of the entire West, was decided by two of its most immature states. For a few weeks in the summer of 1920, the future depended on the performance of a self-taught Polish general commanding an ill-equipped rag-tag of an army and an aristocratic Russian nihilist leading an improvised and tattered yet menacing horde. Reflecting on the resulting struggle a couple of years later, the Polish commander would describe it as 'a half-war, or even a quarter-war; a sort of childish scuffle on which the haughty Goddess of War turned her back'. But this scuffle changed the course of history.[2]

It was itself born of a long history, of a centuries-old struggle between Russia and Poland over who was to control the vast expanses of Byelorussia and Ukraine that lay between them. This was not so much an issue of territory as of Russia's need to break into Europe and Poland's to exclude her from it; yet it had brought

Russian armies into the heart of Poland, and a Polish occupation of Moscow as far back as 1612. The matter had been settled at the end of the eighteenth century by the partition of Poland between Russia, Prussia and Austria and its disappearance from the map. Despite a continuous struggle for freedom and repeated insurrections, Poland remained little more than a concept throughout the next hundred years, and its champions were increasingly seen as romantic dreamers.

But the partition that had removed Poland from the map had also brought her enemies into direct contact, and, in 1914, into deadly conflict. In February 1917, undermined by two and a half years of war, the Russian empire was overthrown by revolution. In October of that year Lenin's Bolsheviks seized power, but their grip on the country was weak, and they were in no position to prosecute the war with Germany and Austria-Hungary. In the spring of 1918 they bought themselves a respite: by the Treaty of Brest-Litovsk they ceded to Germany Russia's Baltic provinces, Lithuania, the parts of Poland under Russian occupation, Byelorussia and Ukraine. A few months later revolutions in Vienna and Berlin toppled the Austro-Hungarian and German empires, which left the whole area, still occupied by German and Austrian troops, effectively masterless. The Poles seized their chance.

Under pressure from President Wilson, the allies had already decided that the post-war settlement should include an independent Poland. They had even granted recognition to a Polish National Committee, based in Paris, which was preparing to form a provisional government. But they had no authority in German-occupied Poland, and no influence at all over the Bolshevik rulers of Russia, whose government they did not recognize. It was clear that the fate of Poland would be decided on the ground rather than in the conference room, and with Russia floundering in her own problems, the Poles, or rather one Pole, took the initiative.

His name was Józef Piłsudski. He was born in 1867 into the minor nobility and brought up in the cult of Polish patriotism. In his youth he embraced socialism, seeing in it the only force that could challenge the Tsarist regime and promote the cause of Polish independence. His early life reads like a novel, with time in Russian and German gaols punctuating his activities as polemicist, publisher of clandestine newspapers, political agitator, bank-robber, terrorist and urban guerrilla leader.

In 1904 Piłsudski put aside political agitation in favour of para-military organization. He organized his followers into fighting cells that could take on small units of Russian troops or police. A couple of years later, in anticipation of the coming war, he set up a number of supposedly sporting associations in the Austrian partition of Poland which soon grew into an embryonic army. On the eve of the Great War Austro-Hungary recognized this as a Polish Legion, with the status of irregular auxiliaries fighting under their own flag, and in August 1914 Piłsudski was able to march into Russian-occupied territory and symbolically reclaim it in the name of Poland.

He fought alongside the Austrians against Russia for the next couple of years, taking care to underline that he was fighting for Poland, not for the Central Powers. In 1916 the Germans attempted to enlist the support of the Poles by creating a kingdom of Poland out of some of their Polish lands, promising to extend it and give it full independence after the war. They persuaded the Austrians to transfer the Legion's effectives, which had grown to some 20,000 men, into a new Polish army under German com-mand, the *Polnische Wehrmacht*. Piłsudski, who had been seeking an opportunity to disassociate himself from the Austro-German camp in order to have his hands free when the war ended, refused to swear the required oath of brotherhood with the German army, and was promptly interned in the fortress of Magdeburg.

His Legion was disbanded, with a only handful joining the *Polnische Wehrmacht* and the rest going into hiding.

They did not have to hide for long. Piłsudski was set free at the outbreak of revolution in Germany and arrived in Warsaw on 11 November 1918, the day the armistice was signed in the west. While his former legionaries emerged from hiding and disarmed the bewildered German garrison, he proclaimed the resurrection of the Polish Republic, under his own leadership.

Piłsudski was fifty-one years old. Rough-hewn, solid and gritty, he invariably wore the simple grey tunic of a ranker of the Legion. His pale face, with its high, broad forehead, drooping moustache and intense eyes, was theatrical in the extreme. 'None of the usual amenities of civilized intercourse, but all the apparatus of sombre genius,' one British diplomat noted on first meeting him.[3]

Piłsudski felt that thirty years spent in the service of his enslaved motherland gave him an indisputable right to leadership. His immense popularity in Poland seemed to endorse this. But that was not the view of the victorious Allies in the west, nor of the Polish National Committee, waiting in Paris to assume power in Poland. After some negotiation a deal was struck, whereby the lion-maned pianist Ignacy Jan Paderewski, who had devoted himself to promoting the cause of Poland in Britain, France and particularly America, and was trusted by the leaders of those countries, came from Paris to take over as Prime Minister, with Piłsudski remaining titular head of state and commander-in-chief. While he allowed Paderewski to run the day-to-day business of the government and its relations with the Allies, Piłsudski continued to direct policy in all essentials. And he had firm ideas on how to ensure the survival of Poland.

The vital question at this stage was, quite simply, the country's geographical extent. Poland's frontiers with Germany and the new Czecho-Slovak state would be decided at the peace conference to be convened shortly in Paris. But her extent in the east would depend on political developments in Russia and the intermediate lands of Lithuania, Byelorussia and Ukraine.

In Russia, the Bolsheviks who had seized power in October 1917 had taken up the German offer of peace in order to concentrate on consolidating their hold, which entailed liquidating all other political factions, on the left as well as on the right. This had allowed the Germans to withdraw troops from the Russian front and throw them into battle against the Allies in northern France, and to make use of the much-needed wheat and oil of Ukraine for a final attempt to win the war in the summer of 1918. Desperate to restore to Russia a government that would resume the war against Germany, the Allies had sent military supplies and even troops to support those Russians opposed to Bolshevik rule who were forming up 'White' armies for the purpose of overthrowing them.

The collapse of Germany and the end of the war in November 1918 allowed the Allies to devote more resources to this aim, while at the same time removing its primary purpose. From now on, Allied support for the Whites took on the character of military intervention in a civil war. This entrenched Lenin and the leading Bolsheviks in their view that the governments of the whole world were ranged against them, and that their only hope of long-term survival lay in toppling the established order worldwide.

The end of the war in the west and the defeat of Germany also meant that Lenin and his comrades had to apply their minds to the subject of Russia's western border. On taking power, they had denounced the eighteenth-century partition of Poland as an act of imperialism and renounced Russia's claim to the areas taken from her. But this did not mean that they intended to relinquish control over them.

The whole area was still occupied by German troops, partly because Germany lacked the means to repatriate or feed them, and partly because the Allies wished them to provide some kind of transitional order. This did not prevent the Bolsheviks from sending in agents who, with the aid of local sympathizers, proclaimed Soviet Republics in Estonia, Latvia, Lithuania, Byelorussia and Ukraine. When the Germans did retire, Russian troops took their place: the purpose was not to set up a string of independent states, but to provide stepping stones for a more important enterprise – the export of revolution.

Karl Marx had only ever envisaged communism working in an advanced industrial society. Its triumph in the backward agrarian economy of Russia had been something of a freak, and to Lenin and his comrades the best way of ensuring its survival appeared to be to export the revolution to Germany. Humiliated by defeat in the Great War, racked by political dissension, awash with unemployed and disaffected soldiers, Germany seemed fertile ground.

Between Russia and Germany lay Poland, a nation that had only just recovered its independence after more than a century of foreign oppression, and was not likely to give it up without a fight. Fervently Catholic and imbued with a patriotism that bordered on religious conviction, the majority of Polish society was impermeable to the most powerful weapons in the Soviet armoury – the lure of socialism on the one hand and the international solidarity of working people on the other. Yet these did hold an appeal for sections of the Polish urban proletariat, for downtrodden or marginalized minorities, and also for many of the Jews who made up some 10 per cent of the overall population; they were mostly extremely poor, underprivileged, often discriminated against, and had little reason to feel any allegiance towards the emergent Polish state over a Russian socialist one. And Poland was in catastrophic condition.

'Here were about 28,000,000 people who had for four years been ravished by four separate invasions during this one war, where battles and retreating armies had destroyed and destroyed again,' wrote Herbert Hoover, who arrived in Poland with his relief mission in January 1919. 'In parts there had been seven invasions and seven destructive retreats. Many hundreds of thousands had died of starvation. The homes of millions had been destroyed and the people in those areas were living in hovels. Their agricultural implements had been depleted, their animals had been taken by armies, their crops had been only partly harvested. Industry in the cities was dead from lack of raw materials. The people were unemployed and millions were destitute. They had been flooded with roubles and kronen, all of which were now valueless. The railroads were barely functioning. The cities were almost without food; typhus and other diseases raged over whole provinces.'[4]

This meant Poland was heavily dependent on the support of her western allies for everything from supplies of food to machine-gun bullets. And while they were generous with this, they were not in a position to help her militarily, even if the will had been there. Lenin guessed that it was not. He and his comrades also believed that history was on their side and that no 'bourgeois' government such as that currently running Poland could possibly stand up to the force of Bolshevism.

Lenin ordered the formation of an Army of the West, which was instructed to carry out 'reconnaissance in depth' in the wake of the evacuating German troops, an operation code-named 'Target Vistula'. On 5 January 1919, after a short battle with a small unit of local Polish irregulars, it occupied Wilno (Vilnius), capital of the erstwhile Grand Duchy of Lithuania, an integral component of the pre-partition Polish state. In February a Soviet Socialist Republic of Lithuania-Byelorussia was set up under Russian protection, with its capital at Minsk, and a Soviet government-in-waiting for Poland was constituted in Russia under the leadership of the Polish communist Józef Unszlicht. The III International of the Communist Party, or Comintern, was scheduled to meet in Moscow on 4 March to watch over the imminent triumph of revolution throughout the world.

An encouraging portent was the emergence that same month of a Soviet government in Hungary under Béla Kuhn, a Hungarian Jew who had become a Bolshevik while a prisoner of war in Russia. But this was short-lived and did not herald further successes. The political situation in Germany stabilized in the spring of 1919, and democratic elections had gone smoothly in Poland, whose 'bourgeois' government was proving unexpectedly vigorous. So was its head of state. As a native of Wilno, Piłsudski could not stomach its occupation by the Bolsheviks, so he gathered together all available reserves and in a daring operation on 20 April Polish troops expelled the Red Army, forcing them back along the whole front and over the next three months occupying most of formerly Polish Byelorussia, along with the city of Minsk.

Piłsudski was determined that while the area lying between Poland and Russia did not necessarily have to belong to Poland, it must be denied to Russia. His favoured scheme was a federation of Poland with democratic Lithuanian and Ukrainian states. This was something of a forlorn hope, since the Lithuanian nationalists who would have been his natural partners were adamant that the whole territory of what had been the Grand Duchy of Lithuania (which included Wilno and all of Byelorussia) be given to them as a precondition of any talks, while the Ukrainians were split between pro-Polish and anti-Polish factions, as well as a variety of Pro-Russian, nationalist and communist groups. But he hoped that some kind of union might yet emerge, and in the meantime determined to occupy as much of the territory of the pre-partition Polish state as possible in order to create a 'safety cushion' and to be in a position of strength when peace negotiations did begin.

The Russian Army of the West had never been intended to fight its way across Poland, only to fill any available power-vacuum. And at this precise moment, the vacuum was behind, not in front of, it. Three White armies, lavishly equipped by the Entente, were challenging the Bolsheviks, from the Baltic in the west, Siberia in the east and Ukraine in the south. The Volunteer Army of Southern Russia, commanded by General Anton Denikin, was beginning to pose a real threat as it began its march on Moscow, inflicting defeat after defeat on the Red Army.

Poland, Germany and world revolution would have to wait. Lenin desperately needed what he called a *'peredyshka'*, a breather, in order to marshal all available forces against this new threat. He therefore decided to repeat the previous year's tactic of buying time with peace, and agreed to secret talks suggested by Piłsudski.[5]

Piłsudski had no illusions about the Bolsheviks. He had personal experience of collaborating with them (he had, at the age of nineteen, supplied Lenin's elder brother with the explosives for the bomb which he had hurled at Tsar Alexander III), and they included a number of Polish socialists with whom he had had close dealings. He was well acquainted with their real aims, and the means they used to achieve them.

But Poland also needed a breather. Her army, a motley collection of units left over from the late war, was badly overstretched – by sporadic fighting in various areas disputed with Germany and not yet allocated by the peacemakers in Paris, by a stand-off with the Czechs over Teschen (Cieszyn), and by a running battle with Ukrainian nationalists over Lwów. More to the point, Piłsudski perceived Denikin as no less of a threat than did Lenin.

The Whites enjoyed the confidence of the Entente, which had just given them millions of pounds' worth of equipment, and had even sent British troops to Russia in support. It followed that if they were victorious Russia would resume her former place as one of the four leading Allies. All Polish territorial claims, indeed her continued existence, would then be entirely conditional on Russia's goodwill.

Piłsudski was being urged by the Allies, and most energetically by the British Secretary of State for War, Winston Churchill, to press on into Russia in support of the Whites. But whatever he may have thought of Lenin and the Bolsheviks, he preferred to deal with them than with a White Russian government, particularly as Denikin had made clear that he viewed the re-emergence of an independent Poland with distaste and regarded most of her territory as Russian. Piłsudski therefore concluded a secret armistice with Lenin which allowed the latter to withdraw some 40,000 men from the Polish front and redeploy them against Denikin.[6]

Within weeks the Red Army was surging southward, triumphantly sweeping Denikin's forces before it. This kind of reversal was characteristic of the Russian Civil War, in which a minor setback would precipitate a retreat that snowballed as technical breakdown, the devastated terrain, the weather, the local population, disease, desertion and fear of political reprisals all conspired to destroy the fabric of the retreating force.

But to politicians and public opinion in the West, it suggested that the Bolsheviks enjoyed the support of the masses and that they were militarily superior, which took away much of the appetite for further intervention in Russia. It also raised fears of unrest at home, fuelled by rose-tinted sympathy for the brave socialist experiment supposedly taking place in Russia. Only the more determined anti-Bolsheviks and the French military pressed for continued intervention.

The British Prime Minister, David Lloyd George, who had been one of the most enthusiastic advocates of crushing the Bolsheviks by force, now declared that Russia would be saved by commerce, affirming that 'the moment trade is established with Russia, communism will go'. Sensing an opportunity, Lenin launched a peace offensive, suggesting negotiations with all parties and offering Poland generous terms. Neither Lloyd George nor the French premier Georges Clemenceau had any intention of making peace with Bolshevik Russia, which they viewed as a dangerous example and a possible source of contagion for the working classes of their own countries. But having failed to destroy the Bolsheviks by military means, they were hoping to contain them. They therefore urged Poland and other states neighbouring Russia to take up the offer. As a result, Poland and Russia entered into official negotiations.[7]

Neither side was in good faith. While the Poles were being publicly urged by Lloyd George and Clemenceau to make peace, they were receiving conflicting messages from other members of the British government and from the French general staff. When Clemenceau resigned, to be replaced by Alexandre Millerand in January 1920, the signals reaching Poland from France were unmistakably warlike. Albeit a socialist himself, Millerand saw his priority as stamping out the strikes paralysing France, and imposing order. This suited Piłsudski, who continued to consolidate his own military position. On 3 January he captured the city of Dunaburg (Daugavpils) from the Russians and handed it over to Latvia, whose government was decidedly anti-Bolshevik and pro-Polish, thereby cutting Lithuania off from Russia. He carried out a number of other operations aimed at strengthening the Polish front, and delayed the peace talks by suggesting venues unacceptable to the Russians.

Lenin was not interested in peace either. He mistrusted the Entente, which he believed to be dedicated to the destruction of the Bolshevik regime in Russia. He saw Piłsudski as their tool, and was determined to 'do him in' sooner or later. He feared a

Polish advance into Ukraine, where nationalist forces threatened Bolshevik rule, and was convinced the Poles were contemplating a march on Moscow. Russia was isolated and the Bolsheviks' grip on power fragile. At the same time, the best way of mobilizing support was war, which might also allow Russia to break out of isolation and could yield some political dividends.

Germany beckoned. The terms of the Treaty of Versailles, signed the previous summer, added humiliation to the already rich mix of discontent affecting German society, and even the most right-wing would have welcomed a chance of overturning the settlement imposed by it. The appearance of a Red Army on its borders would be viewed by many there as providential.

In the final months of 1919 Lenin increased the number of divisions facing Poland from five to twenty, and in January 1920 the Red Army staff's chief of operations Boris Shaposhnikov produced his plan for an attack on Poland, scheduled provisionally for April. This was accepted by the Politburo on 27 January, although the Commissar for War Lev Davidovich Trotsky and the Commissar for Foreign Affairs Georgii Chicherin warned against launching an unprovoked offensive. Accordingly, Chicherin publicly renewed his offer of peace to Poland the following day. Two weeks later, on 14 February, Lenin took the final decision to attack Poland, and five days after that the Western Front command was created.[8]

2

Playing Soldiers

A precondition of the Bolshevik seizure of power in October 1917 had been the destruction of the Imperial Russian Army, which they achieved by systematically undermining every aspect of military service. The first step had been to incite mutiny. They followed this up by encouraging the wholesale murder of officers, by persuading the peasant conscripts to desert and go back to their villages (to 'vote with their feet', in Lenin's famous phrase), and by getting trusted Bolsheviks elected to take command of the remaining troops. Not surprisingly, their attempts to create a new army once they had taken control were hampered by their success in destroying the old one.

As the forces of counter-revolution gathered against them, all the new rulers of Russia could count on were some regular Latvian rifle brigades left over from the Imperial Army and a collection of self-styled Red Guards and detachments of Bolshevik sailors. This motley force combined idealists with criminal elements, professional soldiers with mutineers, students with workers, and Russians with every nationality of the former Russian empire. The overall commander was a former Ensign of the Imperial Army, Nikolai Krylenko.

Desperate measures were called for, and in March 1918 Lev Davidovich Trotsky was appointed Commissar for War to implement them. Trotsky, the epitome of the fastidious intellectual, had no military experience whatsoever, but he was a good organizer. He was also pragmatic. Just as industry needed engineers, he argued, an army needed professional soldiers. He replaced Krylenko with Colonel Ioakim Vatsetis, a Latvian career officer of the Imperial Army, abolished elective command, set up an officers' training school, reintroduced call-up and reasserted the notion of discipline.

While Trotsky did not bring back the old hierarchy of ranks, he introduced a new one, based on the command currently held, abbreviated in the Soviet manner: the commander-in-chief (*Glavnii Komandir*) was titled GlavKom, while commanders of army groups, divisions and brigades were, respectively, KomandArm, KomDiv and KomBrig, and the man in charge of the South-Western Front assumed the less than mellifluous title of KomYug-ZapFront (КомЮгзапФронт).

Brushing aside ideological reservations, Trotsky sought out former Tsarist officers, whom he re-designated from the status of 'enemies of the people' to that of 'specialists'. He would reinstate 48,409 of them in field commands and a further 10,339 in administrative posts over the next two years, with the result that by the spring of 1920 over 80 per cent of the Red Army's cadres would be former Tsarist officers.[1]

This presented a number of problems. Elected commanders who had been demoted to make way for the 'specialists' often took the first opportunity to shoot them in the back. At the same time, many of the 'specialists' proved psychologically incapable of commanding mistrustful, undisciplined troops and adapting to the exigencies of ideological civil war. Others simply looked for the first opportunity to take themselves, and sometimes their units, over to the Whites.

Trotsky resolved these problems by giving each officer a guardian angel in the shape of a political commissar, both to protect him from his troops and to keep him in line. A twin hierarchy of these political officers, beginning with Trotsky himself, who stood behind the commander-in-chief, shadowed every single officer right down to the level of company commander. But while this provided an effective check on unreliable officers and gave the Commissar for War a measure of control over the armies in the field, it did impede military efficiency. It furnished limitless grounds for friction between officers, who resented the implied mistrust and the meddling in military matters, and the commissars, who saw themselves as the effective commanders and sniffed treason everywhere. It was largely thanks to Trotsky's frequent personal intervention that the system worked at all, and with time, even quite smoothly.[2]

Just as challenging for Trotsky was the question of how to recreate the necessary *esprit de corps* and sense of loyalty which the Bolsheviks had so successfully undermined in the former army. His solution was to disband all existing units and feed the men piecemeal into new formations, each of which contained a communist cell loyal to the party, a hard core of committed men who, unlike the conscripted peasants, who were apt to melt away into the countryside, were impervious to the ups and downs of war. The system worked less well in the cavalry: this was largely made up of Cossacks, whose sense of allegiance was volatile at the best of times, with the result that entire units did change sides with astonishing frequency.

For much of 1918 and 1919 Trotsky lived in his armoured train, continually on the move between one front and another, meting out cigarettes, encouragement and threats. In the event, his army proved more resilient and more adaptable in the difficult conditions of the Civil War than the more traditionally structured White armies, which it saw off one by one. But it was about to face a more difficult test, in the Polish army.

Unlike the Red Army, the Polish army was born of tradition. Not the tradition nurtured by most European armies, but one forged in the noble yeomanries of the sixteenth and seventeenth centuries, enriched by the struggles for freedom of the late eighteenth, the Napoleonic wars and the nineteenth-century insurrections. Many Poles had been obliged to fight in the armies of the three partitioning powers during the First World War; others had volunteered to fight, usually under their own flag, either in Piłsudski's Legion or in semi-autonomous Polish formations on the Allied side. But wherever they fought, they clung to the conviction that they were ultimately fighting for their country.

When Piłsudski declared the rebirth of the Polish state in November 1918, the only troops on hand were three regiments of *Polnische Wehrmacht*, a couple of squadrons of cavalry and a pool of cadets, 9,000 men in all. They were soon joined by units, such as the 1st Imperial and Royal Lancers of the Austro-Hungarian army, which were composed entirely of Poles. Within days men from the disbanded Legion and demobilized troops from the Austrian and German armies began to report for duty.

Inevitably, the various units of the nascent army took on the characteristics imposed by the origin of the volunteers. The former legionaries were reconstituted as the first three infantry divisions of the new Polish army, and retained their own ethos. A different kind of force evolved in the formerly German province of Poznań, out of the armed struggle that had broken out between the Poles and the German settlers as both groups returned home after demobilization. By the time the Germans had been ousted from the area, the Polish forces in the province had grown to three divisions. The men, who had all received their training in the German army, had a businesslike approach to soldiering.

The same could not be said of the large numbers of soldiers inherited from the disintegrated Russian and Austrian armies, or the volunteers coming forward from very diverse backgrounds. As well as Poles who had always lived in Poland, there were Poles whose families had lived in exile, sometimes for generations, in all corners of the world. There were also people of many other ethnicities, some polonized, others hardly speaking the language. There were Lithuanians, Tatars, Cossacks, Jews, Germans, Austrians, Hungarians and even many Russians. There were hardened professional soldiers, idealistic students, peasants, aristocrats and socialists. The fact that many were volunteers was a mixed blessing, for while it ensured a high degree of motivation, it also entrenched an element of individualism.

The range was further broadened by the arrival of other existing formations from distant parts. One such was the Siberian Brigade, formed by the Allies out of Poles, mostly prisoners of war, who had found themselves stranded in White-occupied Siberia, which would reach Poland via Japan in 1920. Another was General Żeligowski's division, which had similar origins in the Kuban region of southern Russia, and had, at the insistence of the Entente, briefly fought for Denikin. Another, the most valuable single contribution to the Polish army, was the 'Blue Army'. This had been formed in France in 1917 from Austrian and German prisoners of war of Polish nationality and Americans of Polish origin, recruited in the United States and Canada. It was well trained and equipped, smartly uniformed in French pale blue, and even supported by its own regiment of seventy tanks.

A French military mission of fifteen hundred officers under General Paul Henrys arrived in Poland in the spring of 1919 to train the nascent army on a uniform French pattern. 'Literally everything needs to be rebuilt, from the bottom to the top,' one of them, a young major by the name of Charles De Gaulle, wrote to his mother. A few months later he was forced to admit that the mission was having an insignificant impact. A concurrent British military mission had no real role beyond observation and moral support. Its commander, General Adrian Carton de Wiart, a war hero of Belgian-Irish ancestry who resembled a stage pirate, having lost an eye and an arm, and won a Victoria Cross, in the Great War, was therefore free to indulge to the full his taste for game and wildfowl shooting and his capacity for adventure.[3]

A good example of the state of the Polish army as a whole is provided by a description of the six regiments making up the 1st Cavalry Division, written by an artillery officer attached to it. 'The 8th Lancers were entirely Austrian in character,' he writes. 'Discipline was good, and the regiment's external appearance singled it out from the rest. In no other were the saddles so smartly packed and the stirrups and bits so well polished. The next regiment, the 9th Lancers, was the product of the fusion of the 3rd Lancers of the Austrian *Landwehr* with the 2nd Lancers of the Legion. The fact that most of the officers were legionaries was evident from the external appearance of the regiment. There was less of the lordliness of the 8th and more of a sense of the citizen-soldier; less elegance, but more dash; less training, but more enthusiasm.' The next regiment, the 14th Lancers, was nothing like the other two: the scruffily uniformed men who rode thoroughbred horses on short stirrups and carried lances, sabres and whips tucked into their boots struck the observer as 'a pack of killers of the highest calibre'. Nothing in their bearing or that of their boyish twenty-eight-year-old commander, whom they addressed by his Christian name, betrayed that he was a full colonel and that during the Great War they had all served in the best regiments of the Imperial Russian Cavalry. The 1st Lancers had also served on the Russian side, as an all-Polish regiment. Like the 14th, they carried their lances with the nonchalance of familiarity. They looked down on the 2nd Light Horse, which had legionary origins, and the two regiments disliked each other. The last regiment of the division was the 16th Lancers, recruited in Poznań. 'Its equipment, armament and tack were German. Everything was smart, new and solid. The men all wore tall four-cornered shakos with a triple silver tassel and a red rosette. They also wore Prussian-style uhlan jackets and tall German cavalry boots. Nearly all of them had served in the German army, and it followed that order and discipline were exemplary. They rode huge, bony, heavy horses overloaded with kit. They had everything: sabres and lances, bayonets and spades, gas-masks and canteens. Mounting up was a major performance on account of all this, and when they marched past at a trot, they rattled and clanked like a company of knights.' To the observer, the six regiments were 'like so many children born of the same mother, but conceived by different fathers'.[4]

In the course of the war, cavalry regiments in particular acquired volunteers, either under-age patriots from the minor nobility who had run away from home, or defecting Russians or Cossacks, and these were allowed to serve alongside the regulars. There were also, fighting alongside the Polish army, a number of more or less independent irregular formations. There was a Ukrainian National Army. There was the army of Byelorussia, commanded by General Stanisław Bułak-Bałachowicz, whose own mixed Polish-Lithuanian-Tatar ancestry was reflected in its make-up. There were also a number of smaller units, of Cossacks and anti-Bolshevik Russians.

This pattern of diversity and improvisation was replicated in the Polish officer corps, inherited from various sources. Their training was either Russian, Austrian, German, French or 'legionary'. The obvious differences of language, education and style concealed more fundamental rifts. Each of the various officer schools of the day favoured its own strategic theories, tactical methods and approach to a given situation. As a result, an officer trained in the old German army spoke a different military language to one who had been formed by the Russian Imperial Army, let alone a self-taught legionary officer. That they had all fought on different sides in the Great War did not help. The Poles did have one great asset in the shape of Piłsudski. As head of state and commander-in-chief he could dispense with discussion and follow his own instinct. And while many senior officers found it difficult to defer to an amateur, junior officers and the rank-and-file loved and trusted him. But the lack of a trial period which could have produced greater coherence placed the Polish army at a disadvantage.

While the former Tsarist officers who overwhelmingly led the Red Army may have been ideologically ill-suited, they did all share the same training and background. By the beginning of 1920 most of those intending to desert to the Whites had done so, and the less competent had been weeded out. Those who had come through the trials of the Civil War had proved their loyalty and their ability. The high rate of attrition had also given youth a chance: fronts and army groups were commanded by men in their thirties. The twenty-year-old Vassili Chuikov and the young Georgii Zhukov, both to become marshals in the Second World War, had already been given regiments to command. Semion Timoshenko, another future marshal, was commanding a division at twenty-four.

A similar pattern was discernible when it came to armament. As Poland was unable to produce arms at the time, she could equip her army only with inherited, captured or imported weapons. The Polish infantry were issued with rifles from half a dozen different countries. The Austrian Mannlicher, an accurate but delicate weapon vulnerable to difficult conditions and poor maintenance, was supplemented by German Mausers, British Lee-Enfields, low-quality French war-manufacture and even Japanese rifles. The supply of spare parts and ammunition to this collection severely tested the quartermastership. Units regularly ran out of ammunition and found themselves unable to borrow from their neighbours because they were using different rifles.

The artillery, which was equipped with everything from Canadian howitzers to Italian mountain-guns and antiquated French field pieces, also suffered from supply problems. Strong positions would fall silent at critical moments for lack of ammunition, and if a battery lost its guns it was unlikely to be issued with the same make, and this entailed retraining.

In this respect, the cavalry were the most fortunate. They carried French lances dating from the Franco–Prussian war of 1870 and sabres from a multiplicity of sources, sometimes even the family home, but as long as the weapon was of good quality it could serve in any situation, and if not, a better one could be picked off the body of a slain Cossack.

The Red Army recycled the more up-to-date British and French arms captured from the Whites, but its basic weapon, the Lebel rifle, was of home production. Stocks had been inherited from the Imperial Army, and these were supplemented by a steady trickle from two factories. It was a straightforward, sturdy weapon ideally suited to the treatment it received. It was inaccurate, but this was of minor consequence, as the Russian soldier had little instruction in marksmanship, and anyway relied on the long bayonet which had been the staple weapon of Russian infantry for the best part of two centuries. The weapon that played the most important part in this kind of mobile warfare was the heavy machine gun. While the Poles were equipped with a variety of more or less sophisticated European models, the Maxim prevalent throughout the Red Army was almost unbreakable and could function on a minimum of care.

The Russians possessed as many aircraft as the Poles, if not more, but a shortage of pilots and ground crew, combined with the lack of reliable systems of supply and servicing, kept them on the ground. The Poles, on the other hand, were quick to become airborne, on a variety of old planes left behind by the Germans, as well as Breguet bombers purchased from France and Ballilas from Italy. There was no lack of pilots, as many Poles had served in the Austrian and German air forces in the Great War. These were joined in 1919 by a dozen American volunteer pilots, led by Major Cedric E. Fauntleroy and Captain Merian C. Cooper (who later turned to film-making and both co-directed and flew a plane in *King Kong*). They formed a squadron of their own named after the Polish American Revolutionary War hero Tadeusz Kościuszko. But while planes exerted a powerful psychological influence, and were of enormous use for reconnaissance and to a lesser extent for liaison, they caused little actual damage to the enemy.

Of similarly limited value were the Renault tanks of the Polish army's single armoured regiment. Built to operate over small distances and requiring frequent servicing, they proved a liability for the units they were attached to. The variety of armoured cars used by both sides – Austins, Fords and Renaults supplemented by home-made Polish models and Russian Putilov products – were of greater value, since they combined nearly as heavy firepower as the tanks with far greater mobility.

A useful improvised weapon was the armoured train – usually composed of an engine sandwiched between a couple of armoured railway carriages bristling with machine guns, a couple of trucks or platforms with heavy guns or even tanks on them, and platform cars carrying track-laying equipment. They would be operated by crews of anything up to 150 men, and could carry additional details as required.[5]

The only really successful combination of firepower with mobility was the Russian *tachanka*. This consisted of a heavy machine gun mounted on the back of a horse-drawn open buggy, with one man driving the horses and two manning the machine gun. It could gallop up to a line of enemy infantry, veer round to deliver withering fire at close range, and gallop away, still firing, the moment enemy cavalry or artillery threatened it. Although the Russian infantry made use of the *tachanka*, its prime function was as an adjunct to cavalry, and it helps to explain why and how cavalry emerged as an arm in its own right, and a crucial one, during this war.

The Red cavalry had been formed to fend off the Cossacks, who had joined White armies such as Denikin's in large numbers, and it bore the marks of improvisation. There was nothing elitist or dashing about it: it was composed of renegade Cossacks, former cavalrymen of the Imperial Army and just about anyone who could sit a horse. Its turnout was even shabbier than that of the infantry, and its equipment haphazard. The men wore various items of Imperial Cavalry uniform, embellished at will by baggy red or yellow breeches, captured cartridge-cases and sword-belts, and a variety of headgear ranging from fur caps and Tatar bonnets to peaked or pointed Soviet caps and the odd French helmet taken from a dead White soldier – one witness noted a Russian cavalryman wearing a bowler hat. Some rode on fine Circassian saddles, others on an old rug or cushion. Their basic weapon was the sabre, but each man also carried a carbine of some kind, a revolver, a long knife and a whip, and every troop had a couple of *tachankas* in support.

The Red cavalry's principal strength lay in its uncanny speed of movement and its savage reputation as a kind of latter-day Mongol horde. It marched not in disciplined columns but in loose order, giving the impression of vast numbers on the move, and since it lived off the land, it left behind it a desert, as well as a trail of blood. But the lack of evident discipline hid a kind of organic harmony which gave its movements cohesion and a strong tactical sense when it came to fight.

The Polish cavalry was entirely different in character. It was made up of well trained, mounted and equipped regiments which prided themselves on being elite formations. The numbers were small, no greater than 10,000 fighting men or 'sabres' at the beginning of 1920, as much because of a shortage of good horses as because of the belief widespread following the Great War that cavalry was out of date. But they made up for their small numbers by their skill, and their handling of the lance gave them an edge over the Red cavalrymen.

The cavalry of the respective sides encapsulated the fundamental characteristics of the two armies facing each other: the less numerous Poles relied on smaller, trained and equipped units operating according to established rules of war, the Russians on vast numbers of often entirely unsuitable men, equipped with whatever was at hand, on improvisation and on ignoring received methods in order to exploit any situation. 'The Russian army is a horde,' wrote the man who would lead it into Poland, 'and its strength lies in its being a horde.' This would prove an advantage, given the terrain.[6]

The front across which the two armies faced each other at the beginning of 1920 was over a thousand kilometres long, but only about half of this could be used for military operations; the geographical configuration of the theatre was such that the range of possible manoeuvres was very limited.

The area is shaped like a triangle, with its western angle at Warsaw, and its other two at Smolensk and Kharkov. The northern edge is sealed by a swath of lakelands and forests along what were then the East Prussian, Lithuanian and Latvian borders. The southern side is defined by the Carpathian mountains and the river Dniester, which defined the Czecho-Slovak and Romanian borders. The eastern edge is open to Russia.

The centre of this triangle is taken up by another wedge, the great expanse of bogs, rivers and forests popularly known as the

Pripet Marshes. This means that there are only two corridors along which all east–west movement must pass. The northern one bears the Warsaw–Grodno–Wilno–Smolensk–Moscow road, while the southern one runs from Lublin, through Równe and Zhitomir to Kiev.

Given this topography, it is evident that although it would be possible for one side or the other to press ahead along one of the corridors while remaining passive in the other, it would find its flank exposed if it advanced too far. If it advanced down both corridors, it would be in a problematic position when it passed the central obstacle. Russian armies moving westward down the two corridors would tend to converge and meet somewhere around Brześć or Lublin, while Polish armies would radiate and move away from each other as they progressed eastwards. But the respective advantages and disadvantages of this situation were not what they seemed: the two Russian armies, based on Smolensk and Kharkov respectively, would have to keep operating independently even though their neighbouring units had come into physical contact on the ground. The Polish armies, on the other hand, while appearing to be more vulnerable as they moved eastwards, with a gap being created between them as they passed the Pripet, remained more cohesive, since they enjoyed the common base of Warsaw.

These considerations were given added weight by the distances involved and the nature of the terrain. It is a long way from anywhere to anywhere else, and the scarcity of good roads and towns combined with a profusion of rivers to make that distance problematic. Both Napoleon and Hitler discovered that it is not only the severe winter conditions that can destroy an army: the baking heat of summer and lack of water are just as inimical to the troops, and annul the defensive advantages of most rivers.

There were virtually no metalled roads in much of the area, only tracks that fluctuated between the status of boggy morass and dusty sandpit. Bridges were scarce – over 7,500 had been destroyed by the Germans before they left in 1919. Railways were the only reliable means of getting from one place to another, but the Germans had blown up 940 stations, and the mostly single-track lines were thinly spread over the area. The Poles had inherited three discrete railway networks, built with, respectively, Berlin, Vienna and St Petersburg in mind, which did not mesh comfortably around Warsaw. The Russians used a wider gauge than the rest of Europe, and as that part of their network which was on Polish territory had been converted to suit the others, this meant that with every advance by either side all the tracks had to be converted one way or the other so that supplies could reach the advancing army, unless an adequate quantity of suitable rolling-stock had been captured in the advance.[7]

Means of verbal communication were just as limited. The telephone network was vulnerable to snipping by marauding cavalry. Radio communications were primitive and prone to breakdown. The use of aircraft for the delivery of orders was not favoured, as too many pilots had got lost and touched down in the middle of an enemy grouping. Orders in the field were often carried by mounted galloper. Yet liaison and intelligence were to play a decisive role in the events.

One of the most important weapons in the Bolshevik armoury had always been propaganda, aimed at subverting the population behind the enemy's lines and even the troops in his ranks. Given the nature of the terrain and the scarcity of forces with which to seal its frontiers, Poland was permeable to Russian agents, who spread propaganda and disaffection, and to spies, who sent back information.

While the Poles did not indulge in propaganda behind enemy lines, they did have a valuable network of intelligence agents, mostly Poles stranded in Russia by the Revolution. They had also developed an efficient intelligence-gathering system based on listening in to enemy radio transmission. During the Great War all the combatants had developed receivers that could eavesdrop on the other side's communications, none more so than the Austrians, who found it difficult to obtain intelligence on what was happening on the other side of their eastern front by more conventional means. They invested more resources than any other participant into developing their monitoring technology; and they employed officers of Polish origin, who were both more familiar with the Russian language and had a long tradition of encryption and decryption reaching back through a century of conspiracy and resistance. Polish officers had also served in the monitoring services of the Russian, German and French armies, and as a result the intelligence-gathering unit set up by the Polish army at the beginning of 1919 had a wide knowledge of existing techniques and an unsurpassed range of skills. By the summer of that year it had broken the Russian codes, and by the beginning of 1920 it was listening in to every radio station in western Russia, and intercepting and decrypting 50 per cent of all communications reaching and leaving the Red Army's Western and South-Western Fronts. This was a valuable weapon in what was going to be an unequal contest.[8]

The overall strength of the Red Army at the start of 1920 was five and a half million, which compared favourably with the Polish peak of just under one million. The balance was redressed to some extent as less than one seventh of the Red Army's total were combat effectives, while the Poles managed to put a quarter of their overall strength into the field. The Red Army could only muster seventy operational divisions against the twenty the Poles could field, and they were, if anything, weaker than the Polish ones. That still left a considerable imbalance.[9]

And the millions of men loitering in base camps all over Russia did constitute a vast stock of cannon-fodder which could be fed into the front line when required. So while the Red Army appeared to be incapable of concentrating more than a fraction of its forces against the Poles at any one time, it was able to keep that figure more or less constant. The Poles had no corresponding pool of manpower behind the lines. This meant that the Red Army staked very little in a game in which the Poles were forced to stake all, that it could afford to lose a campaign, while the Poles could not survive the loss of a major battle.

While the Polish army was formed on a conventional modern Western model, it lacked the equipment, the reserves and the technical resources to support it. And it was ill-prepared for the conditions under which it was going to fight. The entire theatre of operations lay well within the developed world and the ambit of European culture, but the infrastructure of modernity was stretched very thinly over it and, like thin ice, was liable to give way under strain, taking with it all vestiges of civilization, and plunging it back into the conditions of the seventeenth century. A soldier trained in the twentieth would suddenly find himself deprived of the support system he had learnt to rely on, operating in a primitive environment populated by an often feral peasantry motivated solely by the instinct for survival.

The Red Army, on the other hand, had grown out of revolution. It had evolved doctrines, strategy and tactics adapted to the worst conditions of the Russian Civil War and to the most exacting terrain. Being the numerically stronger of the two, and because it is easier to destroy a weak order than to uphold it, it was, sooner or later, bound to impose on the Polish army a type of warfare for which the latter was fundamentally unprepared.

The Russian Civil War was a vicious political war, and the rules that govern behaviour in international conflicts do not apply in such wars. Here, there was no room for notions such as respect for the enemy, who was perceived as a form of vermin which must be exterminated. As a result, rank, courage and loyalty, which might earn a soldier the respect of his captors in normal circumstances, only served to make his end more gruesome. This had some curious consequences.

While fanatics stuck to their guns, the majority of combatants caught up in the Russian Civil War saw it largely in terms of personal survival, manifest in a determination not to be on the losing side. Desertion was instinctive when things started going badly. Entire divisions changed sides, and some managed to change back again when the fortunes of war deserted their new ally. This meant that a minor setback, if unchecked, could turn a recently victorious army into a disintegrating rabble within a short space of time.

These conditions heightened tension and fear, which the soldiers of both sides relieved with drink and drugs – thanks to its proximity to Turkey and Afghanistan, the whole of southern Russia was liberally supplied with a wide range of narcotics. They also found relief in almost random brutality. They allayed feelings of insecurity by taking them out on someone else. Whites would do unspeakable things to captured commissars, Reds to officers, landowners or priests. Failing that, there were always the Jews, whom both sides slaughtered with profligacy.

The opponents of the Soviet regime gloatingly pointed to the Jewish origins of Trotsky and other prominent Bolsheviks, which, they claimed, gave substance to the cataclysmic theories contained in the *Protocols of the Elders of Zion*, a grotesque confection purporting to be the blueprint for a Jewish plot aimed at world domination. This did not prevent the Bolsheviks from preying on exactly the same anxieties and prejudices by pointing to the role of Jews in the great capitalist conspiracy to enslave the working class. The poor Jew trying to eke out an existence in some shabby *shtetl* who knew no more of Trotsky than he did of the Rothschilds was guilty by association in the eyes of both sides.

If the war with Poland was not technically a civil war, it was certainly regarded as an ideological one in many respects. The average Red Army ranker was a drafted peasant who might have survived a couple of murderous campaigns of the Great War, then been caught up in the barbarous maelstrom of the Civil War, who did not know what he was fighting for or why, who longed only to go back to his village, who was dressed in rags, covered in lice, suffered from chronic diarrhoea, was perpetually hungry and above all scared, and who expressed his fear and his sense of deprivation by raping and killing anyone he perceived as being with the enemy and defiling anything he could not possess. Priests and landowners unwise enough to remain in the path of the Russian advance were tortured and butchered, and the large Jewish population of the borderlands fell victim to much the same fate as their brethren in Russia, notwithstanding that they mostly welcomed the Red Army. Polish officers and those identified as volunteers were usually hanged or shot on capture, often after being tortured and having various parts of their body such as nose, ears, tongue and genitalia cut off.

While the Polish high command struggled to inculcate the principles of the Geneva Conventions in their men, their writ did not run very far in the field. And their behaviour deteriorated markedly as the contest grew more bitter and more critical. Captured commissars were often hanged, soldiers suspected of having committed atrocities shot, and, following the recapture of territory briefly occupied by the Red Army, those deemed to have collaborated, which usually included the Jewish population, roughly dealt with.

3

Grand Designs

The plan approved by Lenin in January 1920 envisaged the concentration of overwhelming forces on the Western Front, to the north of the Pripet. These were to launch the offensive, supported by the armies of the South-Western Front in Ukraine. Operations, originally scheduled to begin in April, were delayed by the need to disengage units from the fight against the remnants of Denikin's forces in the Caucasus and transfer them to the Polish theatre. This gave the Poles a chance.[1]

Piłsudski was keenly aware that if Russia were allowed to mobilize her full potential the Polish army would be swamped. He was therefore determined to win the race for the spring offensive and to knock out one or other of the Soviet fronts facing him. The other could then be contained without too much trouble. As a preliminary measure, he ordered General Władysław Sikorski's* army group to take Mozyr, which drove a wedge between the two Russian fronts and would provide a pivot for the next Polish offensive, whether it took place in the north or in the south.

---

* One of the founders of Piłsudski's fighting squads, briefly Prime Minister of Poland in 1922–23, politically active in opposition to Piłsudski in the 1920s and 1930s, Sikorski would become Polish Prime Minister and Commander-in-Chief in 1940, and effective war leader of the Poles until his death in a plane crash off Gibraltar in 1943.

Intelligence gathered from intercepts of Russian orders revealed to Piłsudski not only that the Russians placed no more faith than he did in the peace talks, which duly broke down in April over technicalities; it also indicated that while the Russians were building up their forces both north and south of the Pripet, the main thrust would come in the north. Piłsudski nevertheless decided to deliver his first strike in the south, for two reasons. One was that as spring came earlier in Ukraine than in Byelorussia, operations could begin promptly and be over by the time the Russians were ready to strike in the north. The other was that this would permit him to indulge a cherished dream.

When the Bolsheviks had occupied western Ukraine at the end of 1919, the Ukrainian National Army of Ataman Symon Petlura had been obliged to seek refuge in Poland. Piłsudski meant to help Petlura re-establish himself and create a Ukrainian state friendly to Poland. The Polish–Russian frontier would be halved as a result, and the Poles could then concentrate on defending the northern corridor. He calculated that if he struck soon, Petlura could have consolidated his position in Ukraine by July, which would free all Polish forces for the anticipated Russian offensive in the north.[2]

On 25 April one Ukrainian and nine Polish divisions under the direct command of Piłsudski launched an offensive against the Russian South-Western Front in Ukraine, commanded by KomYugZapFront Aleksandr Yegorov, a remarkable man of twenty-seven who, in spite of his peasant origins, had attained the rank of lieutenant-colonel in the Imperial Army. Piłsudski's intention was to destroy the two Red Army groups strung out along the front by sending cavalry deep into their rear to cut off their retreat by capturing the rail and road junctions of Korosten, Zhitomir and Koziatyn, while superior forces attacked them from the front. The plan worked perfectly. General Romanowski's cavalry brigade

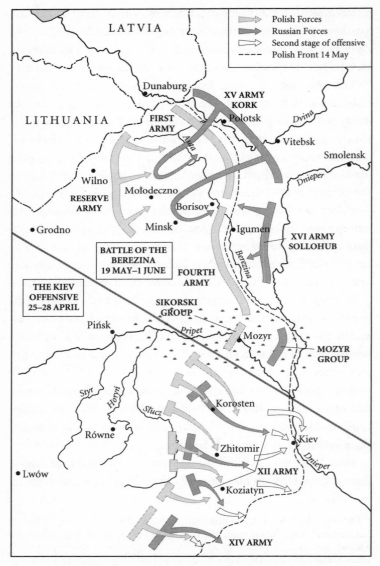

	Polish Forces
	Russian Forces
	Second stage of offensive
- - - -	Polish Front 14 May

LATVIA

Dunaburg

XV ARMY KORK

LITHUANIA

FIRST ARMY

Polotsk

Dvina

Vitebsk

Smolensk

Wilno

RESERVE ARMY

Mołodeczno

Dnieper

Borisov

Minsk

Igumen

XVI ARMY SOLLOHUB

Grodno

Berezina

BATTLE OF THE BEREZINA 19 MAY–1 JUNE

FOURTH ARMY

THE KIEV OFFENSIVE 25–28 APRIL

SIKORSKI GROUP

Pińsk

Pripet

Mozyr

MOZYR GROUP

Styr

Horyń

Słucz

Korosten

Równe

Zhitomir

Kiev

Dnieper

Lwów

XII ARMY

Koziatyn

XIV ARMY

The Kiev offensive and the battle of the Berezina

seized Korosten the following morning, while another cut the Russian retreat at Zhitomir, and on the morning of 27 April the 1st Cavalry Division took Koziatyn after a two-hundred-kilometre march. But the results were not as Piłsudski had anticipated.

The two Russian armies facing him were in no condition to resist a vigorous attack. KomandArm Sergei Mezheninov's XII Army consisted of undermanned and poorly led units strung out along a shallow arc more than 250 kilometres long, some two hundred kilometres west of their headquarters at Kiev. To the south, the front was held by the smaller but more efficient XIV Army of the talented twenty-four-year-old Lithuanian Bolshevik Komand-Arm Ieronim Uborevich. Together, the two armies mustered no more than 20,000 men, and possibly less. Both forces were kept busy defending their supply lines from a low-level guerrilla war carried on by Ukrainian partisans, and on the eve of the Polish offensive two of Uborevich's brigades deserted to join Petlura.*3

When the Poles and Ukrainians launched their attack, supported by armoured cars and aircraft, the Russian front gave way, and by the end of the second day of the offensive the XII and XIV armies were in full retreat. This was to save them. The Polish cavalry which had taken up positions astride their lines of retreat were too weak to stem the resulting flood of men, most of whom had jettisoned everything in their haste. As a result, almost two-thirds of Mezheninov and Uborevich's effectives managed to slip through Piłsudski's carefully laid trap.

Piłsudski was convinced the Russians would do everything to defend Kiev. He therefore decided to halt his advance in order to

---

* These brigades, made up of men from western Ukraine, had been part of the Austrian army during the Great War, at the end of which they had fought against the Poles for possession of Lwów, subsequently joined Petlura, and, when his luck ran out, Denikin's White Army, from which they had switched to the Reds.

let them rally their forces while he prepared a second attempt at annihilating them. He despatched two cavalry groups to cross the Dnieper to the north and south of the city and encircle it while he concentrated his main forces for a frontal attack. He meant to begin this on 9 May, but on 6 May the Polish cavalry brigade which had crossed the Dnieper and approached Kiev from the rear found the city undefended. The following morning Polish and Ukrainian troops marched in without firing a shot.

The Russians had indeed intended to defend Kiev. On 1 May the Supreme Commander (GlavKom) Sergei Sergeievich Kamenev had issued orders that the city be held at all costs, at the same time taking measures to reinforce Mezheninov. The first reinforcements, a brigade of Bashkir cavalry, had arrived on 5 May. Mezheninov's own account has his XII Army taking up new positions before Kiev and putting up a fight before being obliged to fall back in the face of a fierce attack by superior Polish forces. In reality, they abandoned their positions as soon as Polish troops approached.[4]

It was, on the face of it, a triumph for the Poles. In just under two weeks they had defeated two Soviet army groups, taken over 30,000 prisoners, captured huge quantities of materiel, moved the front forward by some two hundred kilometres and occupied the strategically and politically important capital of Ukraine. Everything had gone like clockwork. Even Major De Gaulle was impressed. 'The sense of manoeuvre, of threatening the enemy's flanks and rear, is very highly developed in the Polish Army,' he wrote in an official report.[5]

But Piłsudski admitted to feeling uneasy. The operation had failed in its purpose. He had damaged the two Russian armies, but they had saved themselves by flight, and could be operational once more as soon as their losses had been made up. At the same time he had committed almost half of his forces to defending a vast tract of territory, and they would soon be needed elsewhere.

His only hope lay in Petlura successfully raising an army able to take over the defence of the area. But Ukraine had been bled by six years of war, its civil society destroyed by no less than fifteen different regimes in the space of three years as Tsarist rule had been followed by Austrian, German, Bolshevik, White and Polish administrations of one sort or another, punctuated with a variety of Ukrainian regimes. There was correspondingly little confidence in Petlura's ability to survive, and an attendant lack of commitment. His forces, which had numbered 12,000 at the outset, never grew much above 30,000, and his government struggled to form an adequate administration.[6]

Piłsudski's failure to achieve his military objective was nothing to the blunder he had committed in diplomatic terms, which was to have severe repercussions on the further course of the war. And he had played into the hands of the Bolsheviks, who gained immeasurably, both at home and on the international scene.

When the plans for her invasion were being discussed back in January 1920, Chicherin had warned of the necessity of provoking Poland into making the first move, so the Soviet government could represent itself as acting in self-defence when it launched its offensive. Piłsudski's attack had been a godsend in the circumstances. World opinion had forgotten that there was a war on, and that by repudiating the eighteenth-century treaties of partition the Soviet government had recognized the whole area up to the Dnieper as Polish, and nobody had much time for the Ukrainians. The Polish offensive therefore appeared to the outside world as an unprovoked invasion of Russia.

The day after the Poles entered Kiev the *New Statesman* of London was voicing the opinion that it was 'impossible for anyone who is concerned for the future peace of Europe to hope for anything but an early disaster for the Polish armies'. The following day a communist 'Hands off Russia' committee called for a boycott, the consequence of which was that dockers in the port of London refused to load a shipment of arms bound for Danzig (Gdańsk). A week later, the Executive Committee of the Communist International sitting in Moscow issued the following manifesto:

> *Transport workers, railwaymen, dockers, seamen! Do not dispatch supplies or food to Poland, for it will be used in the war against workers' and peasants' Russia. German railwaymen! Do not pass trains through from France to Poland. Dockers of Danzig! Do not unload ships destined for Poland. Austrian railwaymen! Not one train must get through from Italy to Poland.*[7]

It was not just socialists and workers who ranged themselves against Poland. Large sections of world opinion swung against it, and the Entente distanced itself. The British and French governments were irritated by Piłsudski's unilateral action. Lloyd George was incensed, and even anti-Bolsheviks such as Churchill were annoyed that he had struck now and not in the previous year, when he could have saved Denikin.

Piłsudski's offensive had also inadvertently cast the Soviet regime in the role of Russia's champion against perceived foreign aggression, thereby boosting its legitimacy at home, and the Bolsheviks found themselves riding a wave of national outrage at the Polish occupation of Kiev, considered to be a shrine of Russian history and culture. An appeal for volunteers yielded thousands, including many former officers who had baulked at joining the Red Army in order to fight the Whites, but were more than happy to serve against the Poles: in Moscow alone, 1,500 of them came forward in the space of a week amid strident calls for national unity in the face of the enemy.[8]

This would prove invaluable to the newly appointed commander of the Western Front, KomZapFront Mikhail Nikolaievich

Tukhachevsky, one of the more eye-catching personalities in the Red Army. He was twenty-seven years old, with a slim figure, swarthy complexion and lank dark hair reminiscent of the young Napoleon. But Tukhachevsky, a nobleman by birth, had an innate elegance and refined, slightly epicene looks. His biographers endow him with lineages that include aristocrats, peasants, Italians, Tatars, a crusader and even Genghis Khan, and he certainly played upon such suppositions by indulging in behaviour calculated to shock.

He had set off to war in 1914 as a lieutenant in the elite Semeonovsky Foot Guards, and was decorated for bravery no fewer than six times in as many months, before being taken prisoner in 1915. After five failed escape attempts he was incarcerated in the high-security fortress of Ingolstadt. There he befriended a number of French fellow prisoners, whom he drove to depths of melancholy by playing mournful pieces on his violin and shocked with his provocative pronouncements: after a lengthy discussion on literature, he would declare that all books should be burnt so that the soul of man could be truly liberated. One day a French captain found him building a grotesque cardboard monster holding a bomb, which he explained was the God of War and Destruction, Pierun. 'We will enter into the state of Chaos, and will only emerge from it with the total ruin of civilization,' Tukhachevsky solemnly told the astonished Frenchman as he prostrated himself before it.[9]

His nihilism had an unpleasant tinge to it. 'The Jews brought us Christianity, and that is reason enough to loathe them,' he lectured on another occasion. 'And anyway, they belong to a low race. You cannot understand this, you Frenchmen for whom equality is a dogma. The Jew is a dog, son of a bitch, and he spreads his fleas throughout the world. It is he who has done more than any other to inoculate us to the plague of civilization, and who would like to give us his morality, the morality of money, of capital...The great socialists are Jews, and the socialist doctrine is a branch of universal

Christianity...I loathe all socialists, Christians and Jews!' But he would not let such antipathies stand in his way. 'Why should I care whether it is with the Red Banner or the Orthodox Cross that I conquer Constantinople?' he mused. He never tired of reading about or discussing the feats of Caesar and Napoleon, and was determined to be, in his own words, a general or a corpse by the age of thirty.[10]

Tukhachevsky finally succeeded in escaping from Ingolstadt in 1917, and made his way back to Russia. On reaching Moscow he offered his services to Trotsky, who gave him command in Siberia, where he stopped and eventually rolled back the White army of Admiral Kolchak. He was then transferred to the Southern Front to take charge of the mopping-up operation against Denikin. His posting to the Western Front in April 1920 opened up grandiose vistas to his imagination and possibilities to his military talents. He was to lead the Red Army in its first international war.

Tukhachevsky would have liked to build up his forces gradually and wait for the promised reinforcements to arrive, but Kamenev ordered him to attack immediately so as to relieve pressure on the Ukrainian sector. He had a slight numerical superiority over the Poles, with 115,000 men to their 95,000, and this was compounded by the fact that the Polish forces were strung out in a thin line along the whole length of the front, with only a small reserve stationed behind it.[11]

Tukhachevsky resolved to pin down the Polish Fourth Army by delivering frontal attacks on Borisov and Igumen with KomandArm Nikolai Sollohub's XVI Army, while his main force, KomandArm Avgust Kork's XV Army, advanced in a south-westerly direction towards Mołodeczno and then wheeled round to drive the Polish First Army into the rear of the Fourth, pushing both back on to the Pripet Marshes, where they could be destroyed.[12]

The Russian attack began on 14 May, a week after the Polish capture of Kiev. The Poles were taken by surprise, and the First

Army was forced back on Mołodeczno. But the attackers failed to build up sufficient momentum to carry through Tukhachevsky's plan, and soon ground to a halt. At this point the commander of the Polish Northern Front, General Stanisław Szeptycki, a capable soldier with years of distinguished service in the Austrian army and subsequently as commander of Piłsudski's Legion, rallied the First Army and, with the support of a reserve army rapidly cobbled together by General Kazimierz Sosnkowski,* on 1 June pushed Kork's XV Army back. The Poles advanced along the whole front, and the Russians began to retreat in disorder. Morale collapsed and whole units surrendered – a cavalry brigade consisting of two regiments, the 'Thunder of Victory' and the 'Unvanquished', surrendered en masse to a single troop of Colonel Władysław Anders' 15th Lancers.† Szeptycki was for pressing home his advantage, but he was reined in by Piłsudski and ordered to create a new front line along the rivers Auta and Berezina. The reason for this was that Piłsudski needed to take troops from the Northern Front in order to stabilize the situation in Ukraine, which had taken a turn for the worse.[13]

While Petlura struggled with the recruitment and training of the Ukrainian army that was to take over from the Poles, fresh complements of men and whole units were arriving to reinforce the Russian front facing them. This was to be not only reinforced, but also transformed into an offensive force, by the addition of the 1st Cavalry Army, *Piervaia Konnaia Armia*, Konarmia I for short. This had been formed by Trotsky in the previous year as a foil for the White Cossacks, and had already achieved legendary status, largely thanks to its commander.

---

* Sosnkowski, a firm supporter of Piłsudski and his political tradition, would succeed Sikorski as Polish commander-in-chief after the latter's death in 1943.
† As commander of the Polish 2nd Corps in World War II, Anders would distinguish himself in the Italian campaign of 1944, particularly at Monte Cassino and Bologna.

Semion Mikhailovich Budionny was a tall, well-built man of forty with a theatrical moustache and a swashbuckling manner. He was semi-literate and obtuse, but he was brave, cunning and a born survivor. He was also a fine horseman, with many years' service in the Imperial Cavalry, in which he had attained the rank of corporal. He joined the Bolsheviks in 1917, but Trotsky had few illusions about him. 'Wherever he leads his gang, there they will follow,' he said, 'for the Reds today, tomorrow for the Whites.' Budionny's political commissar, Kliment Efreimovich Voroshilov, was a close associate of the increasingly influential young Stalin, Lenin's Commissar for Nationalities, and the three had become friends during the defence of Tsaritsyn (later Stalingrad) against Denikin. By the time Tukhachevsky arrived to take command of the Southern Front in 1919, this 'Tsaritsyn circle' consisting of Stalin, Voroshilov and Budionny had established its influence, and flouted his authority openly. Stalin was now commissar to the South-Western Front, so Voroshilov and Budionny had a friend where they needed him.[14]

By the spring of 1920 the Konarmia had grown to four divisions of horse, which between them could muster 18,000 'sabres', a brigade of infantry, fifty-two field guns and countless *tachankas*. It also possessed five armoured trains, eight armoured cars and a squadron of fifteen planes. The latter were largely irrelevant, as two of the pilots flew their craft over to the Polish side at the first opportunity, while the rest were captured by a Polish raid.[15]

Budionny's tactics were simple: he would approach an enemy position, grope about until he found the weakest spot, and apply the massed strength of all four divisions to it. He would smash his way through by sheer weight of numbers and then, without looking to left or right, dash into the enemy's rear, where his men would fan out to spread devastation and panic. At this point the breached front usually collapsed and the enemy units began a headlong retreat which the Konarmia would turn into a rout. Budionny hated dismounting his men or attacking positions frontally. He avoided contact with enemy cavalry, and when a confrontation could not be avoided, the Konarmia's usual tactic was to tempt the other side to charge and then veer off to the side, leaving its *tachankas* to deal with them.

The Konarmia's strength lay in the speed with which it could move and its ability to instil fear, and its men nourished its mystique by howling and whistling as they charged, by their wanton destruction of everything that lay in their path, and by their massacres of prisoners and civilians. 'This swarm of horsemen would raise gigantic dust-clouds on the horizon, blotting out everything for miles around and giving the impression of a great, fast-moving and fantastic force pouring into every available space, and finally kindle a feeling of utter impotence in the enemy ranks,' in the words of one Polish cavalry officer.[16]

Budionny was to play a key role in the plan drawn up jointly by Yegorov and Kamenev, who came down to South-Western Front headquarters at Kharkov. The intention was to destroy the main Polish force around Kiev, the Third Army under General Edward Śmigły-Rydz, one of Piłsudski's most faithful legionary stalwarts. Mezheninov was to tie it down by attacking the bridgehead it had established on the east bank of the Dnieper while two flanking groups folded back its wings. Budionny was to pierce the Polish front further south, then veer round into its rear. Once the Third Army had been destroyed, the Konarmia was to spearhead an attack by the XII and XIV Armies on Równe and Lublin.[17]

On 26 May Budionny began to probe the point at which Śmigły-Rydz's Third Army and General Antoni Listowski's Sixth Army met. He bore down on the 7th Division, which made up the tip of the Third Army's right wing, and threw it back in

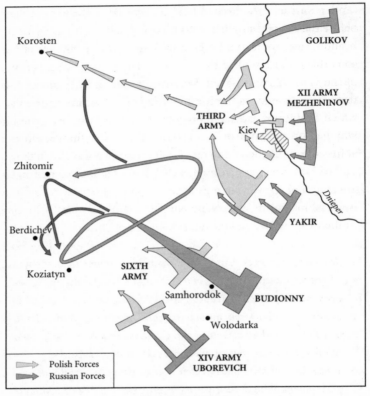

The Kiev débâcle

disorder. But as he began to advance into the gap he had made in the Polish front, he was confronted by the Polish 1st Cavalry Division.

It was a difficult moment for its commander General Aleksander Karnicki. As he had held high rank in the Tsarist army before the Revolution, Piłsudski had despatched him to Denikin's headquarters when the Entente had insisted that he send a liaison officer. Karnicki had thus been a witness to the disintegration of the White Army and the Konarmia's role in it. To make matters worse, he had, as the commanding officer of the regiment in which Budionny had served before the Great War, been the one who had promoted him to corporal. With fewer than 3,000 men at his command, he was to face his former corporal's 18,000.

The two forces confronted each other near Wolodarka on the afternoon of 29 May, in a kind of encounter that had been banished from Europe with Napoleon. 'The sun was already dipping in the west,' records a Polish lancer:

> The 1st Krechowiecki Lancers deployed to the left and began to move up the slight incline at a trot in the direction of the Bolsheviks. As we came over the ridge, we caught sight of a huge wave of Budionny's cavalry descending from the opposite ridge into the dip, also at a trot. The Bolsheviks had the setting sun in their eyes, and probably could not make out the strength of their opponent. Both sides slowed to a walk and came to a standstill facing each other. A colourfully-dressed rider galloped out of the swarm of Cossacks on a magnificent black charger and, waving his sabre above his head, shouted:
>
> 'Well, my Lords! I'm Cossack Kuzma Kruchkov. Who'll take me on?' At this, a murmur ran along the row of officers standing in front of the 1st Lancers. 'Racięcki! Yes, Racięcki!' Captain Racięcki (the best swordsman in the regiment) passed his sabre to his left hand to make the sign of the cross with his right and then began to move

towards Kruchkov at a walk. Kruchkov sprang towards him at a gallop. Racięcki parried the first cut, aimed at his head, and himself slashed fiercely to the right and down, cutting Kruchkov open from the collar to the waist. At this, a howl went up among the Cossacks. 'He's dead! Dead! The Devil!' they shouted, and the whole lot turned tail as our regiment began to charge…

We moved off at a gallop, arched low in the saddle, lances at the horse's ear, sabres raised high for the cut. A man who has not been through the emotions of a cavalry engagement can never know the exhilaration and frenzy experienced by the charging horseman. Nerves are stretched to breaking-point, the fear one might have felt vanishes, while the horse, warmed by the passion of the rider, carries him at a wild gallop, frenzied and ready to trample or bite.[18]

Budionny was taken aback, and withdrew to ponder his next move. The Polish cavalry was not the only problem on his mind. Two days later, a brigade of Don Cossacks belonging to his 14th Division shot their political officers and went over to the Poles. On 1 June Budionny made another attempt at breaking through the Polish front, but after two days' fighting he was once again forced to retire.

Mezheninov, whose XII Army had been pounding the Polish defences around Kiev, was doing no better. His left wing, an assault group under the command of KomDiv Iona Yakir, a twenty-four-year-old graduate of Basel University and one of the few Jews to hold high rank in the Red Army, had been equally unsuccessful. Yakir had two infantry divisions, a special brigade from Moscow and a cavalry brigade under KomBrig Grigorii Kotovsky, a veteran revolutionary. He was a large man resplendent in yellow fur-trimmed tunic and red cap with a reputation for extravagance and savagery, whose equally flamboyant men were famed for skill and bravery. Yakir was nevertheless unable to make headway against the Polish defences, and was even badly mauled by a task force of Śmigły-Rydz's legionaries.[19]

The only one of Mezheninov's forces to make any progress was an assault group under the twenty-year-old future marshal Filipp Golikov, consisting of the 7th and 24th 'Iron' Divisions and the Bashkir Cavalry Brigade, a formidable combination of red caps, oriental faces and curved sabres, which had managed to cross the Dnieper to the north of Kiev and taken the first step in the encirclement of the Poles.

On 5 June Budionny at last managed to break through the front at the juncture of the Polish Third and Sixth armies near Samhorodok and swept into the Polish rear. There followed ten days of chaotic operations, in the course of which both sides lost a chance of doing serious damage to the other. The Polish front closed up behind Budionny, and since the other sectors of it were holding firm, he was in a trap. But to take advantage of this situation, the Poles needed unity of command and coordination in the field, neither of which they could deliver: Piłsudski had reorganized the front command twice within the past couple of weeks, and the attendant confusion was compounded by poor communications. Budionny for his part was in a position to close the ring around Kiev and seal the fate of the Polish Third Army. But instead of marching east towards Kiev, he sent two divisions off to raid Zhitomir and Berdichev, while the other two moved not east, but west, on Koziatyn.

The raids on these key points in the Polish rear did extensive damage and spread panic, but they were strategically pointless. Kamenev's orders were that Budionny cooperate with Mezheninov's forces in the destruction of Śmigły-Rydz's Third Army at Kiev. Budionny's immediate superiors, Yegorov and Stalin, were, for reasons of their own, more interested in the destruction of the Polish Sixth Army. They assumed that having cut the Third Army's lifelines and sowed chaos in its rear by the raids on Zhitomir and Berdichev, they could leave its final annihilation to Mezheninov, and therefore sent Budionny into the rear of the Sixth Army so as to cut that off. But the Polish cavalry not only prevented Budionny from penetrating into the Sixth Army's rear, but drove him back to Koziatyn in a series of epic cavalry engagements.

Having failed to cut off the Sixth Army, Budionny at last turned about and moved east, to seal the fate of the Poles in Kiev. He would still be in time. On 10 June the Konarmia made contact with Yakir's group, which had folded the Polish front back on itself. But at this point Budionny received fresh orders from Yegorov and Stalin, to leave the Poles at Kiev to Mezheninov and Yakir, and go back and have another go at Koziatyn.

That same day Śmigły-Rydz at last began to evacuate Kiev. But instead of moving directly westwards to sandwich the Konarmia as he had been ordered, he retreated along the Korosten railway line. Once he had brushed aside Golikov's forces, he was free. The Kiev encirclement had failed to materialize. Yegorov and Stalin belatedly ordered Budionny, who was by now outside Zhitomir, to veer north and cut off the Polish retreat, but he was tied down by Polish cavalry and could spare only two divisions, which he duly despatched under the command of Voroshilov. These not only failed to intercept Śmigły-Rydz but suffered at the hands of the Polish rearguard. To make matters worse, Budionny was himself attacked vigorously by the Polish 1st Cavalry Division. He was not pleased. Nor was Kamenev, whose orders had been flouted. But heads did not roll, because Stalin had covered his tracks by cabling Lenin with a distorted version of events that deflected the blame from himself and Yegorov on to Kamenev.[20]

That the Russians had failed to achieve their aims was of little comfort to the Poles. By the end of June they had been forced back

The Polish commander Józef Piłsudski reviewing volunteers setting off for the front.

The Russian commander-in-chief (GlavKom) Sergei Sergeievich Kamenev with soldiers of the Red Army.

Russian infantry on parade.

Russian heavy artillery outside Warsaw, August 1920.

A colour party of Red cavalry, spring 1920.
The Red cavalry's secret weapon, the *tachanka*: a Maxim gun mounted
on a sprung buggy provided the best combination of mobility and
firepower in difficult terrain.

Polish field artillery on the market square of Pińsk, spring 1920.

The Polish 16th Lancers marching through Równe, March 1920.

Polish heavy artillery in Ukraine, May 1920.

The Polish Air Force's Kościuszko Squadron, made up of American volunteers. Its commander, Major Cedric E. Fauntleroy, is fifth from the left. At his right hand is Captain Merian C. Cooper, aka the director of *King Kong*.

The Polish General Lucjan Żeligowski, the product of the Imperial Russian Army, a tough and resourceful divisional commander.

KomDiv Iona Yakir, a graduate of the University of Basel and one of the few Jews in the higher reaches of the Red Army, was in command of two divisions at the age of twenty-four.

The Polish armoured train *Śmiały*.
Both sides had dozens of such trains, which came in all shapes and sizes.

KomandArm Ieronim Uborevich, a Lithuanian Bolshevik, was one of the few army group commanders who had not been a professional officer of the Russian Imperial Army.

General Kazimierz Sosnkowski was, like Piłsudski, a product of conspiracy and subversion, and received his military training in the Polish Legion.

A Russian divisional radio transmitter. This cumbersome and unreliable piece of equipment provided the only means of communication in the field for larger units, and added an element of unpredictability to the operations.

A Russian Austin armoured car produced by the Putilov works, captured by the Poles in the Kiev offensive and pressed into service under a new name.

General Edward Śmigły-Rydz taking the salute as Polish troops march into Kiev, 7 May 1920.

to where they had started on 25 April. They had lost a great many men and horses, and much equipment. The troops' faith in traditional military virtues had been shaken by the tactics of the Red Army and its uncanny resilience (one cavalry officer likened trying to defeat the Konarmia to beating a feather bed with a stick). And a new kind of fear had taken hold. As they retreated through areas ravaged by Budionny's raiding parties, they saw evidence of what they could expect if they were caught. Desertion rose exponentially.

Śmigły-Rydz, who had taken over command of the Polish South-Eastern Front, managed to halt the retreat and take up positions similar to those before the start of the offensive. As his forces dug in, Piłsudski wrote to Szeptycki on the Northern Front that 'there will be no further withdrawal on the Ukrainian Front'. But Budionny could not afford to hang about. On 26 June he found an undefended spot and broke through. Once again the whole Polish front trudged back, to the line of the river Horyń.[21]

Although a new defensive line was rapidly formed, it was clear that Piłsudski had lost the initiative, and in a desperate bid to recover it, he decided to destroy the Konarmia, whose importance as a psychological factor he belatedly recognized. He therefore took the risk of further weakening his forces in the north in order to put together a force that could deal with Budionny decisively. He stripped Szeptycki's northern front of its remaining cavalry and combined this with the remnants of the 1st Cavalry Division and a reinforced Second Army, which he put under the command of General Kazimierz Raszewski, formerly a colonel of hussars in the Prussian army.

But Budionny did not wait for the new operational group to form up, and on the night of 2 July the Konarmia crossed the Horyń, making for Równe. The Polish cavalry were caught unawares, and the 3rd Legionary Division, which was supposed to be defending the town, abandoned it without a fight. Its commander, General Leon Berbecki, a good example of the ex-legionary officer's attitude to others, could not be bothered to inform 'that Prussian Raszewski', who was vainly trying to locate the various elements of his operational group.[22]

Budionny swept into Równe, taking men and equipment, and set up his headquarters there – at the Hotel Versailles, no less. But his triumph was short-lived. Raszewski managed to rally Berbecki's division and locate his dispersed cavalry, and launched an assault on Równe from the north and west, while another division, the 18th Marcher Rifles, attacked from the south. On 8 July Berbecki's 3rd Division fought its way into Równe, nearly capturing Budionny himself in the process, while the 18th began cutting off two of the Konarmia's divisions. But before the trap could be closed Raszewski received orders to break off the action and fall back to the line of the river Styr, a hundred kilometres further west.

On 11 July Budionny was back in Równe, counting the spoils of victory. He had taken thousands of prisoners and valuable supplies. He had also sown fear throughout the area. But his triumph over the Polish forces ranged against him was more apparent than real. The reason they had disengaged and fallen back to the Styr was that Tukhachevsky had again struck in the north, and Piłsudski needed every available soldier there.

Tukhachevsky had been building up his forces throughout June. Existing units were brought up to strength and reinforced by the arrival of new formations, many of them, such as the 33rd Kuban and the 27th Omsk Rifle Divisions, renowned units hardened in the campaigns of the Civil War. Kork and Sollohub kept their commands, Evgenii Sergeyev, who had commanded one of Kork's divisions during the battle of the Berezina, was promoted to lead the new IV Army, while KomandArm Vladimir Lazarevich arrived to take command of the new III Army and Tikhon Khviesin to command the Mozyr Group, a smaller force designed to cover the Pripet Marshes. They were all 'specialists' who had reached the rank of full colonel in the Imperial Army, except for Khviesin, who was a barber from Saratov.

Possibly Tukhachevsky's most useful acquisition was the 3rd Cavalry Corps, Konkorpus III, consisting of two divisions of horse and an infantry brigade. Although half the size of the Konarmia, it was to play an even more pivotal role, thanks largely to its commander. Gaia Dmitrevich Bzhishkian was an Armenian born in Tabriz, Persia, in 1887. He changed his name to G.D. Gai in 1914 when he was drafted into the Russian army, in which he saw service against the Turks. In 1918 he formed a Red Guard detachment in Samarkand. He fought his way through areas controlled by the Whites and joined Tukhachevsky's Army of Siberia in Samara. He commanded a division and then an army group before being given the task of forming a Circassian cavalry corps for Tukhachevsky to fight Denikin. Gai was no cavalryman, but he was far more intelligent than Budionny, and more adroit in his use of cavalry as a spearhead for infantry. And he cultivated an aura of Asiatic ferocity so successfully that he was generally referred to as Gai Khan.[23]

By the beginning of July Tukhachevsky could muster some 120,000 men, with many more in reserve. This gave him an almost twofold superiority over Szeptycki, who disposed of somewhere between 60,000 and 80,000 men. Bearing in mind that the latter were strung out in a thin line along a six-hundred-kilometre-long front while Tukhachevsky could choose where to concentrate and strike, there could be no doubt that he would break through the Polish front with ease. Morale among the Polish troops, who had been stuck out in this melancholy landscape of forest and bog for a long time, was low, and desertion on the increase. Tukhachevsky's men by contrast were being intensively prepared and motivated for the forthcoming offensive.*[24]

Tukhachevsky followed a plan similar to that adopted in May: to encircle and annihilate the Polish First Army, thus outflanking Szeptycki's other two armies, which he would then drive sideways into the Pripet Marshes. But this time he was taking no chances. He concentrated three of his armies, nearly 100,000 men, in the north against the First Army, 36,000 strong. And to make sure the Poles would not be able to pull back and re-form a defensive line, Gai's Konkorpus would bypass the First Army to the north and lunge deep into the enemy rear.[25]

Tukhachevsky was expected to take Warsaw by 12 August, which gave him six weeks in which to cover nearly seven hundred kilometres. This meant he could not afford to stop and fight any set-piece battles along the way. He must break through and keep going as fast as he could. Such tactics had worked against Kolchak and Denikin: the enemy force had melted away during the retreat, while the attacking one had been able to make up for losses by incorporating deserters and volunteers, and for supplies left behind in the rapid advance by seizing jettisoned enemy materiel. Tukhachevsky did not admit of any difference between the White armies and the Polish one, and assumed that the Polish state would crumble in the face of the Russian advance, for he saw this war entirely in ideological not national terms. On 3 July the following order was read out in all companies, squadrons, platoons and batteries of the Russian Western Front:[26]

---

* The 33rd Division (15,000 men) was subjected to eleven meetings, one hundred reading sessions, 1,000 discussions, twenty-five lectures, 104 cell meetings, thirty-seven general meetings and twenty 'spectacles', all in the space of three weeks.

SOLDIERS OF THE RED ARMY!

The time of reckoning has come. In the blood of the defeated Polish army we will drown the criminal government of Piłsudski.

Turn your eyes to the West. In the West the fate of World Revolution is being decided. Over the corpse of White Poland lies the road to World Conflagration. On our bayonets we will bring happiness and peace to the toiling masses of mankind.

The hour of attack has struck! Westwards!

On to Wilno, Minsk, Warsaw – Forward!

Early the following morning Tukhachevsky's artillery opened up on the positions of the First Army as Sergeyev moved forward at the northern tip of the front. He was to pierce the Polish line, let Gai through and then attack in a south-westerly direction. Gai was to cover forty kilometres on the first day, and Sergeyev twenty-five. But the Polish line proved more difficult to break than expected, and it was not until late afternoon that the Russians were through. Kork and his XV Army had also met with stiff resistance from two Polish divisions, the 10th and 17th, under General Lucjan Żeligowski, a former professional soldier in Tsarist service who had later commanded a Polish division under Denikin. Only Lazarevich, further south, had made any headway, cutting the Polish front in two and advancing some ten kilometres.

Although they had held their own surprisingly well, the Poles were in an untenable position, and Szeptycki ordered a general retreat to the line of German Great War trenches, a hundred kilometres to the rear.

Apparently convinced that the First Army had been shattered, Tukhachevsky put into operation the second phase of his operation, thereby allowing the Poles to get away. Instead of pursuing

Map labels: SWEDEN; DENMARK; BALTIC SEA; Niem...; Danzig; EAST PRUSSIA; 6 Aug; Lc; Ostrołęka; Berlin; Poznań; Vistula; GERMANY; Warsaw; POLAN...; Prague; Kraków; Vistula; C Z E C H O S L O V A K I A; Vienna; AUSTRIA; Budapest; HUNGARY

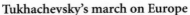

Tukhachevsky's march on Europe

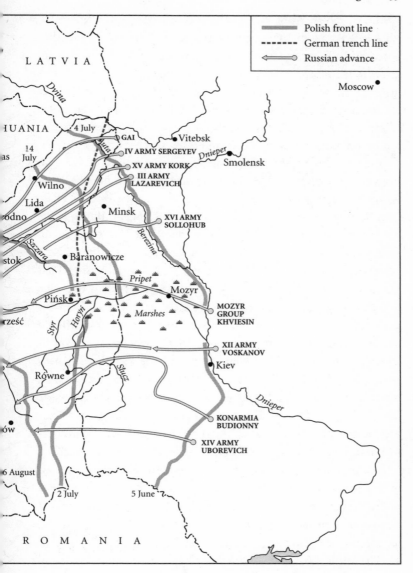

▬▬▬▬	Polish front line
- - - - -	German trench line
⟵○	Russian advance

Moscow

LATVIA

Dwina

LITHUANIA

4 July

GAI

14 July

Vitebsk

IV ARMY SERGEYEV

Dnieper

Smolensk

Wilno

XV ARMY KORK

III ARMY
LAZAREVICH

Lida

Minsk

Grodno

XVI ARMY
SOLLOHUB

Szczara

Berezina

Białystok

Baranowicze

Pripet

Mozyr

Pińsk

MOZYR
GROUP
KHVIESIN

Marshes

Horyń

Styr

Brześć

XII ARMY
VOSKANOV

Kiev

Słucz

Równe

Dnieper

KONARMIA
BUDIONNY

XIV ARMY
UBOREVICH

Lwów

16 August

2 July

5 June

ROMANIA

them, Sergeyev, Kork and Lazarevich wheeled south into what should have been the rear of the Fourth Army and Sikorski's Group, but since these had also begun their retreat, the Russian pincers encountered nothing bar a few stragglers. Tukhachevsky's prize for three days' fighting was 3,000 prisoners and sixteen pieces of artillery. He nevertheless reported to Kamenev that the Polish army had been 'totally smashed' and was 'fleeing in complete disorder, leaving behind prisoners and other trophies'.[27]

On 12 July the retreating Poles reached the line of German trenches, but no sooner had they begun to dig in than Gai's Konkorpus skirted their positions and clattered into Wilno. There was nothing the Poles could do but pull back again. But now the Polish retreat was beginning to resemble flight, and the Russian advance gained in speed. A few days after the fall of Wilno, Tukhachevsky's advance guards caught up with the retreating First Army outside Lida and inflicted defeat on it. Szeptycki drew his front back to the line of the rivers Niemen and Szczara.

This new line faced north-east, with its northern tip anchored on the fortress of Grodno, its centre at Baranowicze and its southern tip at Pińsk. In an attempt to exploit the fact that his own forces had drifted southwards in the retreat while the Russian spearheads, which had reached Grodno, were far ahead of the rest, Szeptycki decided to mount an attack in a northerly direction from Baranowicze to cut them off. But while he was preparing his attack, on 19 July, Gai fought his way into Grodno, making mincemeat of Szeptycki's plans as well as of the garrison. The First Army retook the fortress, but after fierce fighting Gai was once more master of the place on 24 July. Sergeyev and Kork crossed the Niemen in several places, and the Poles streamed back to the next natural line of defence, along the rivers Bug and Narew.

The fall of Wilno on 12 July had caused alarm in Poland, and played into the hands of Piłsudski's enemies, who vociferously denounced his strategy. A new Government of National Defence was formed under the Peasant Party leader Wincenty Witos. This was politic, since the advance of the Red Army into Poland raised the possibility of social unrest. The Bolsheviks had been conducting active propaganda in Poland for over a year, inciting workers and peasants against the 'Polish Lords', persuading them to join the great international of the downtrodden, and holding out dazzling prospects of a socialist paradise if they did. While this kind of propaganda found fertile ground among the urban proletariat, its appeal to the rural population was limited. But the war was unpopular with the peasants, particularly the landless ones, who might yet be swayed. In order to scotch this, the Polish parliament, the Sejm, unanimously voted in a land reform bill on 15 July that would redistribute land from large estates to the landless.

The new government also issued an appeal for help to the Entente. Neither Britain nor France wished to get involved, but they felt they had to do something, so they took two steps, neither of which was to have any influence on the course of events. The first was a telegram to Moscow despatched by the British Foreign Secretary Lord Curzon, suggesting a ceasefire along a 'minimum Polish frontier' sketched by himself and a peace conference in London.* The Russian response was predictable. Chicherin questioned the right of the Entente, which was still waging war on Soviet Russia through the agency of the Whites, to mediate a peace.

The Soviet leadership felt understandably embattled, and viewed Poland predominantly as a tool of the Entente. Curzon's proposals appeared to them little more than an attempt to buy time in order to prepare a future onslaught on Russia from Polish

---

* This would later become notorious as the 'Curzon Line', and provide endless grounds for argument in the inter-Allied negotiations of 1943–45.

territory. They also feared that if they rejected the peace proposals outright the Entente might, anticipating the fall of Poland, feel it necessary to go as far as to arm Germany against them. At the same time, the Franco-British response demonstrated that the Entente was unwilling to come to Poland's aid directly. Lenin calculated that it was therefore safe to continue the offensive, while agreeing to direct peace talks with Poland. He consequently ordered Yegorov and Tukhachevsky to speed up the offensive on both fronts.[28]

The other measure taken by the Entente was to send an Inter-Allied Mission to Warsaw, consisting of Lord D'Abernon, a former Member of Parliament and one-time financial adviser to the Egyptian government; the French author and diplomat Jean Jules Jusserand; Generals Hacking and Maxime Weygand, and a number of others. These distinguished gentlemen turned up in Warsaw, where they conferred with ministers, generals and ambassadors, held emergency meetings and shook their heads disapprovingly. Much of their energy was directed at trying to place Weygand in command of the Polish army. Weygand, who had been Marshal Foch's chief-of-staff, and was widely believed to be the natural son of the ex-Empress of Mexico Carlotta or King Leopold II of the Belgians, enjoyed enormous prestige. But Piłsudski was not impressed. 'How many divisions have you brought?' he is reputed to have asked him at their first meeting, turning away in contempt when the Frenchman admitted he had none. In an effort to repair hurt pride Weygand was eventually appointed assistant chief-of-staff by Piłsudski.

Piłsudski had no intention of relinquishing command. It was not in his nature to do so: he had created the current crisis, and, being honourable as well as obstinate, he felt it was up to him to resolve it. The situation looked grim, with the Polish armies retreating at the hint of a Russian advance and the rate of desertion spiralling upwards. But Piłsudski was not as intimidated as most observers, and the half-hearted response of the Entente only served to harden his determination.[29]

He replaced Szeptycki, who was ill and discouraged by his recent experiences, with General Józef Haller, the respected former legionary and later commander of the 'Blue Army' in France. He reinforced the front along the Bug and Narew and instructed Haller to hold it at all costs. He meant to make another attempt to defeat Budionny, which would permit him to transfer forces from the south and use them to launch an attack on Tukhachevsky's flank from Brześć, which was being held by Sikorski.

It was a sensible plan. Budionny's spectacular advance had begun to run out of steam. His greatest assets – speed and mystique – had been eroded by the need to slow down and fight. After the initial reactions of panic and desertion, the Polish troops facing him had steadied and become battle-hardened. 'We have no reserves, we are too weak to defend ourselves, so we can only attack,' noted a lieutenant of the 1st Legionary Infantry in his diary on 29 June.[30]

This was not what Budionny and his men had anticipated when they began their invasion of Poland. They had been told that they were being sent to liberate the Ukrainian and Polish workers from the 'Polish Lords', and had expected to be received as heroes. They had also been led to believe that they would be marching through a land rich in the luxuries of 'bourgeois' life.

In the event, they found themselves having to fight every inch of the way against determined troops who were self-evidently not all 'Polish Lords'. Their march took them through poverty-stricken countryside ravaged by years of war, dotted with villages made up of squalid hovels and ramshackle towns populated mainly by Jews. While some of the younger peasants and Jews welcomed and even joined them, most viewed them with puzzled apprehension. There was little food to be had, and not much in the way of 'bourgeois' luxuries, only flies, dirt and ruination. What they did find they destroyed, smashing beehives to get at the honey and chopping down apple trees to get at the fruit. They desecrated and defiled churches and country houses, in which they could find little worth taking (the universal calling card of a visit by Red soldiers was shit – on furniture, on paintings, on beds, on carpets, in books, in drawers, on plates). They also looted shops, often leaving most of the booty, which was of no use to them, outside in the dirt. As well as killing obvious 'enemies of the people' such as priests and landowners, they also raped and murdered civilians at random. Their officers insisted that they treat the Jews with forbearance, but once night fell, there was no stopping the rapine. They also massacred prisoners of war, often just for their boots or their uniforms. They were depressed and morale was not good, and they were also sick. Many suffered from dysentery and, according to the writer Isaac Babel, who was attached to the political unit of Pavlichenko's 6th Division, every single one of them had syphilis.[31]

From Równe, Budionny made for Łuck, first swerving south towards Brody with the intention of outflanking the Second Army and taking the town from behind. But he failed to break through the front with sufficient force, and the wings of the two Polish armies were bent back rather than snapped. They sprang back at his flanks like a pair of swing doors as he advanced. 'We were being hemmed in,' records Babel. 'For the first time in the campaign we could feel on our backs the devilish lash of flank attacks and blows from behind – a taste of the very weapons that had served us so well.'[32]

Budionny halted his advance and diverted two divisions of his own and an infantry division borrowed from Yakir to deal with the threat to his left flank, which came from Krajowski's 18th

Marcher Rifles, entrenched at Dubno. General Franciszek Kraj-owski was, at fifty-nine, a little old to be commanding a unit in the field. He was a Czech career officer in the Austro-Hungarian army who had made Poland his home after 1918 and volunteered his services. He had been given one of the most decrepit divisions, the tail end of Haller's 'Blue Army'. In a matter of weeks he had turned it into one of the steadiest and toughest. He held cavalry in contempt, and thought Budionny a joke. He taught his men to form squares and shoot horses at close range, which discour-aged the Cossacks from approaching, and stuck to his positions with all the obstinacy of age. After a few days of vain efforts, on 19 July Budionny brought the entire Konarmia, reinforced by Yakir's 44th Rifle Division and the prestigious 8th Red Cossack Division led by the twenty-three-year-old Vitalii Primakov (a fer-vent Bolshevik who had taken part in the storming of the Win-ter Palace), over six divisions in all, to bear against Krajowski's one. A ridiculous encounter ensued as he attempted to batter the entrenched and determined Poles with one frontal assault after another. 'I manoeuvred with regiments and brigades, trying to probe the weakest spot in the enemy's defence – all in vain,' he wrote. 'Everywhere, the enemy hung on stubbornly.'[33]

Timoshenko, commander of the 6th Chongar Division, even-tually skirted the Polish positions and found a gap through which to threaten their rear, and Krajowski was obliged to fall back on Radziwiłłów. But as soon as Budionny tried to resume his advance, on 22 July, Krajowski was on the offensive again, this time as part of a concerted attempt by the Second and Sixth Polish Armies to cut the Konarmia in half. But while Krajowski thrust deep into its flank and reached the point at which he was to join up with his opposite number from the Second Army, in this case the 6th Kraków Division, the latter never showed up. The attempt was repeated several times over the next few days, but the

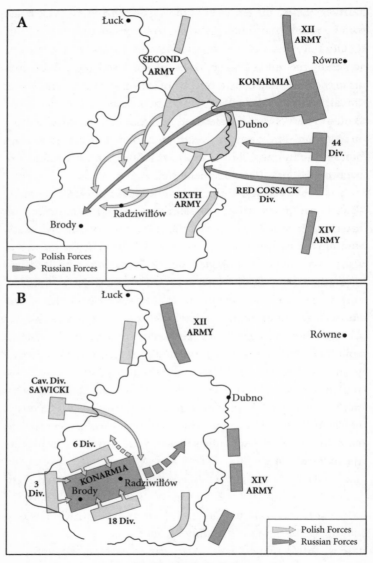

The Battle for Brody

northern Polish pincer never managed to join up with Krajowski, and Budionny continued his advance as far as Brody.

On 1 August the two divisions cutting into his flanks were joined by the 3rd Legionary Division, which began to harry him from the front, and by two freshly formed cavalry divisions which threatened the Konarmia's rear. 'The vermin are choking us,' Budionny was heard to exclaim. On 3 August he gave the order to abandon Brody and fall back on Dubno. But his retreat was blocked by the two Polish cavalry divisions, and his chances of breaking out of the encirclement looked slim.[34]

The Polish cavalry, under the command of General Kazimierz Sawicki, were preparing to attack the retreating Konarmia when Sawicki received an order to break off all action and withdraw in a northerly direction. After some hesitation – victory was in sight – he reluctantly obeyed, and instead of destroying or at least mortally wounding the Konarmia, the Polish cavalry withdrew, suffering some losses as it disengaged from the Cossacks desperate to break out of the encirclement.

The order had come from Piłsudski: on the night of 1 August Sollohub's XVI Army had launched a violent attack on Sikorski's positions at Brześć, and after a less than inspiring defence, disrupted by fifth-column action, the town had fallen. The Russians were across the Bug, and the fourth and last line of defence before Warsaw had been breached. The defence of the capital had become the priority, and all available troops would be needed for the battle ahead.

4

The Miracle on the Vistula

If the Russian capture of Wilno had shaken the confidence of the Poles, the fall of Brześć three weeks later came as a real shock. People could not understand how it was that, having broken through a front some six hundred kilometres away, Tukhachevsky was, only four weeks later, approaching Warsaw, and without having actually won a battle. 'This is not war – there are no corpses!' reflected an astonished De Gaulle. 'Divisions advance and retreat without anyone knowing why.' A sergeant of the 42nd Infantry did know why. 'The fighting had an insidious quality, since there were no trenches in which to take up positions,' he wrote. 'One had to expect an attack from any quarter, and in consequence the fighting was bloodthirsty, as you either won or you perished – our men were just as cruel as the Bolsheviks. Human life lost all value…We knew that death was waiting for us at every turn, because the Bolsheviks either killed outright, or drew out the torture as long as they could.' But even he admitted that there was something incomprehensible about the relentless Russian advance. 'If anyone could have seen this wave of Bolsheviks advancing on us, they would have been astonished, on account of their appearance,' he goes on, 'as some were barefoot, others wore bast leggings, others some kind of rubber confections, and they wore a variety of headgear, even ladies' hats, winter caps and kerchiefs, or nothing at all, with their hair in the wind. They were like weird apparitions.' The inexplicable nature of this extraordinary threat gave it an uncanny quality. 'Something like the kingdom of AntiChrist is moving upon the whole Christian World,' wrote the Russian philosopher Dimitrii Merezhkovsky. A kind of resigned fatalism began to make itself felt throughout the country.[1]

'This incessant wormlike movement by large numbers of enemy troops, punctuated now and again by a sudden leap forward, a movement continuing for weeks on end, gave the impression of something irresistible rolling on like some heavy, monstrous cloud,' wrote Piłsudski. 'There was something about it that destroyed hope, broke down the inner qualities of men and the resistance of armies. For the military, this advance was like a horrific kaleidoscope, producing a fresh picture every day, in which new geographical names, numbers of regiments and divisions jostled with new time-factors and calculations of distances. Although this kaleidoscope revolved slowly, the relentless monotony of its movement gave rise to a chaotic jumble of unfinished counter-measures, unfulfilled orders and outdated reports, all totally irrelevant to the new situation as it crystallized.' And if Tukhachevsky's 'beautiful march', as Piłsudski called it, reduced the Polish staff to mesmerized impotence, its effect on the rank-and-file was devastating.[2]

The First Army, which had made up the northern tip of the Polish northern front, had been assailed by overwhelming forces on the first day of the offensive. While it had stood its ground well, it was nevertheless obliged to retreat. And as it was continually outflanked by Gai's cavalry each time it tried to halt and catch its breath, this retreat had become so precipitate that it had turned into flight. Many of the senior officers were not up to coping in such conditions, while command structures were too fragile to hold together what was still a fledgling army. Younger officers panicked or gave way to defeatism, and some were so haunted by the fear of what might befall them on capture that they stripped their uniforms of all insignia of rank.[3]

All this did nothing to reassure the men. On account of the vastness of the area to be held and the meagre forces available, they operated in battalions, companies or platoons which often had no immediate contact with their neighbours. This meant that they could never be sure whether the units on either side were holding their position or not, and the nagging fear that they had been left behind in an isolated position combined with the terror of capture to undermine all attempts at making them hold firm. While many deserted outright, the majority merely retreated as fast as they could, often ahead of their units. By 19 July, only eleven days into the retreat, the 5th Division of General Jędrzejewski's group could muster only five hundred fighting men, while about four times that number of its soldiers were a day or two's march ahead, clogging up roads and railway stations, cadging rides on supply wagons, and often ditching equipment in the process.[4]

Jędrzejewski's neighbour, General Żeligowski, one of the toughest and most popular generals in the Polish army, managed to keep a tight grip on his two divisions. His 10th, dubbed 'Żeligowski's Iron Division' by the Whites when it had served with Denikin in 1919, had borne the brunt of the fighting when Tukhachevsky launched his offensive on 4 July, yet its retreat, which at seven hundred kilometres would be the longest of any Polish unit, was orderly and defiant throughout. But even its soldiers were affected by the general psychosis. 'Six weeks of consistent backward movement created a sort of compulsion to retreat,' wrote Żeligowski. 'The soldier thought about it when he went to sleep, and it was his first thought on waking. It assumed the character of a disease, and its germs entered every bloodstream. During those long weeks we withdrew after every engagement, regardless of whether we had won or lost; it was not cowardice, or despondency, or lack of determination, more of a habit that had warped every mind. This habit was the most dangerous of all; where and when and under what conditions would it be possible to overcome it?'[5]

Conditions were gruelling. 'The road of retreat is infernal,' noted a soldier of the 37th Łęczyca Infantry. 'The heat, the lack of water, the stench of rotting corpses and the forest fires are turning it into a sort of hellish torture...Continual shooting from the flank and rear...' The men had worn out their boots and uniforms. Food was irregular and insufficient. As it was summer, the villages they passed through could provide only milk, rotten potatoes and unripe fruit, causing colic and diarrhoea. Civilian refugees clogged the already crowded roads, increasing the disorder and spreading panic. The shortage of cavalry on the Polish side added to the sense of isolation and insecurity of the infantrymen as they trudged back, and every unit or group of men developed the same survival reflexes as the deserter. The pace of the retreat was such that, according to Sikorski, a dozen soldiers of his group actually became demented from exhaustion.[6]

The worst effects of the retreat, however, were to be felt hundreds of kilometres behind the front, or, in Piłsudski's words, on 'the most dangerous front of all – the internal front'. Horrified by the rapidity of the retreat and increasingly doubtful as to whether it could be stopped, Polish society was on the brink of panic. European opinion had more or less given up on Poland. The London *New Statesman* reported that 'the Polish Army seems for the time being almost to have ceased to exist as a coherent force'. Foreign embassies evacuated their personnel, and as the military attachés called on General Haller to take their leave they shook his hand 'like that of a bankrupt cousin', as he put it.[7]

The Soviet leadership had taken much the same view. It looked as though they were going to be able to destroy 'bourgeois' Poland before they were obliged to make peace with it. Accordingly, on 23 July Lenin created a Polish Revolutionary Committee, Pol-RevKom, in effect a Soviet government for Poland, consisting of the veteran Polish communist Julian Marchlewski, the dreaded founder of the Russian Secret Police (Cheka) Feliks Dzierżyński, the Jewish communist Feliks Kon, Edward Próchniak and Józef Unszlicht, to take power once Warsaw had fallen. The same afternoon, Kamenev issued fresh orders from the Red Army field headquarters at Smolensk urging Tukhachevsky to press home his advantage with all speed and to take Warsaw without delay. A week later, on 30 July, the PolRevKom took up residence in a magnificent palace outside the Polish town of Białystok.

Trotsky urged caution, but few listened. Delegates to the Communist International sitting in Moscow were in paroxysms of excitement as they watched the flags showing the positions of the Red armies move forward every day on the huge map that hung on the wall. World revolution seemed within reach. On 23 July Lenin wrote to Stalin raising the possibility of a thrust through Romania, Czechoslovakia and Hungary with the aim of staging a revolution in Italy. In his reply, Stalin agreed that 'it would be a sin' not to try.[8]

Their enthusiasm blinded them to the realities of the situation at the front, which was far from being as rosy as appeared from the flagged-up maps. Tukhachevsky had moved the whole western front forward by five hundred kilometres in the space of five weeks, defeating two Polish army groups in the process and shattering the entire Polish system of defence. This sustained advance was not only a remarkable feat of arms, but also an extraordinary triumph of organization and logistics. Tukhachevsky had provided his four army groups with 30,000 peasant carts, and these were supplemented by requisition from every town and village his troops passed through. He took care to rebuild bridges and to adapt the railway tracks as he moved forward, managing to convert them to the Russian gauge to within eighty kilometres of Warsaw. This was a remarkable achievement given the poor technical resources of the Red Army and the speed of his advance.[9]

But this had all been achieved at immense cost in organization and effort, and every part of Tukhachevsky's army was beginning to feel the strain. His experience of the Russian Civil War suggested that the land through which his armies moved could provide them with supplies and make good his losses in men. But the nature of this campaign was radically different. Although it was not difficult to find enough communist sympathizers and disaffected young men to form local militias to cover the rear of the Red Army, few viable recruits came forward from the villages of Byelorussia and even fewer in Poland, and there was no real possibility of incorporating Polish prisoners or deserters into it. At the same time, the long march through increasingly hostile territory had not only thinned his forces, but also cooled much of their patriotic ardour. Tukhachevsky tells us his men were 'strong in spirit and did not fear the enemy', but he was in Smolensk.

KomDiv Vitovt Putna, the young Latvian-born former Tsarist NCO and now commander of the 27th Omsk Rifle Division, tells a different story. 'There were signs of great weariness in our troops,' he writes, 'the condition of the armies, and particularly of their rear, was a source of very serious alarm to me.' The parish priest of a small Polish town was less than impressed as he watched the Red Army march in. First came a galloping Cossack, shooting wildly, accompanied by a civilian commissar. 'Then came the infantry, which inspired pity, since most of the men were barefoot,' he writes, 'some wore civilian clothes, others the uniforms of various armies, mostly Polish ones, presumably from stores left behind by us in Byelorussia or taken from prisoners. One's heart ached at the sight of this famished and tattered mob...'[10]

Like almost every other Russian commander, Tukhachevsky would later claim that he had wanted to pause on the line of the river Bug, catch his breath and make good his losses before embarking on the final stage of the operation, the capture of Warsaw. There is no evidence to support this claim. Not surprisingly, since having built up such momentum it would have been madness on his part to throw away his main advantage and give the Poles a chance to recover themselves and regain the initiative. However tired his army might have been, logic demanded that he continue to move forward with all possible speed.

At the same time, continued advance would not only add to its exhaustion; it would, as he passed the Pripet, expose his left wing. Anticipating this, he had already requested Kamenev to transfer to his command the forces of the South-Western Front operating in Poland – the Konarmia and the XII and XIV Armies.

This was logical, and not only because Tukhachevsky's left wing was now vulnerable. The South-Western Front was aimed at the Crimea, the Balkans and south-central Europe, yet its right wing was being drawn westwards into Poland, thereby extending it and redirecting its effort elsewhere. It would not get to Italy by way of Lublin. So it was incumbent that those of its armies operating in Poland be transferred to an extended Western Front, as Tukhachevsky wanted, otherwise they would naturally drift southwards. But nobody at South-Western Front headquarters would willingly hand over three armies, and nobody, least of all Stalin, liked the idea of playing second fiddle to Tukhachevsky. If he was going to have the glory of taking Warsaw and bringing the Revolution to Germany, Stalin and Yegorov could console themselves with Lwów, and possibly Budapest, Vienna and even Rome. So while Kamenev issued the appropriate orders, Yegorov ignored them.[11]

In fact, the Konarmia and the other two armies of the South-Western Front operating in Poland, the XII, now under

KomandArm Gaspar Voskanov, and Uborevich's XIV, no longer represented any great military value. The long march from the Crimea, the heavy fighting during and just after the breakthrough in Ukraine on 5 June, the rapid advance, made more difficult by constant skirmishing with Polish cavalry and by the increasingly confident sorties of the Polish infantry, and finally the gruelling two-week battle of Dubno-Brody, had sapped the strength and undermined the morale of the Konarmia.

The very nature of the fighting had changed in the past weeks: the terror tactics that proved so effective in the unstable conditions of the Russian Civil War and in Ukraine, where the Poles felt exposed in a potentially hostile environment, had given way to more regular fighting, as the Polish infantry gained confidence and learned to defy terror with steel. Its resolve hardened with every step the two sides took nearer the Polish heartlands. This kind of fighting was not what the Konarmia had been intended for, and it had been all that Budionny and Voroshilov had been able to do to keep it from cracking under the strain. 'The troops had reached the outer limits of human endurance,' Budionny wrote; 'everywhere people were collapsing with exhaustion, unable to move.' He even claimed the horses were so tired they lacked the energy to swish their tails at the flies.[12]

Budionny and Voroshilov hardly slept during the battle for Brody, galloping from one threatened sector to another, exhorting and leading by example. When Sawicki's cavalry closed off its retreat it looked as though the Konarmia might disintegrate as a force. And although it was saved by the Polish withdrawal, it was in no state to continue fighting. 'Fully aware of its responsibilities, the Revolutionary War Council of the Konarmia declares that notwithstanding the political demands of the day, the Konarmia cannot be expected to do what is beyond its power,' Budionny cabled Kamenev. 'In the interests of saving the cavalry, which may one day be of use to the Soviet Republic, we insist that you approve the immediate tactical withdrawal of the Konarmia...'[13]

Without waiting for a reply, Budionny fell back and called a rest. Supplies and reinforcements were called up from the rear, and in order to invigorate the exhausted men and presumably to check any repetition of a recent desertion of another five hundred Don Cossacks to the Polish side, the political officers embarked on a rigorous programme of 'party-political' and 'cultural-enlightenment' activity, consisting of newspaper readings, reading lessons and 'discussions on the internal and international position of the Soviet Republic'.[14]

It would need more than this to put the fight back into the Konarmia, without which the other two armies of the South-Western Front were toothless. It required a proper rest and considerable reinforcement. And, having fallen behind, the Konarmia would need up to a week to catch up with the armies of the Western Front. Unless Tukhachevsky paused for a couple of weeks, there was no way in which it could play a part in the operations around Warsaw. And this was not going to be the walkover that Tukhachevsky, who had taken up residence in a country house outside Smolensk, where he passed the evenings with wine, women and his violin, or Lenin, surrounded by eager communists from all over the world, had begun to take for granted.[15]

Despite breaching the last defensive line before Warsaw on 1 August, Tukhachevsky's armies were not able to surge forward as before. Żeligowski's group, by now no more than a skeletal force of hardened veterans, fought a desperate rearguard action in the marshy Narew basin, in the Ostrołęka–Łomża–Ostrów triangle, which kept Kork's XV and Lazarevich's III Armies pinned down for six whole days. 'This was our first serious delay,' wrote Tukhachevsky, who took it to be a planned counterattack by the main Polish forces. At the same time Sollohub's XVI Army, which had crossed the Bug and taken Brześć, was caught in a vigorous counterattack by Sikorski and thrown back across the river.[16]

It was not until the end of the first week in August that Tukhachevsky was able to resume his westward march. When he did, his armies began to close in on the Polish capital. In the north, Gai and Sergeyev had met no serious resistance and were consequently far ahead of the other armies. This extended Russian pincer hanging over Warsaw looked ominous on the map, and seemed to preclude the Poles forming a new defensive front. But this apparent advantage concealed the fundamental shift that had taken place in the strategic positions of the two armies.

Tukhachevsky's plan had been predicated on the destruction of Szeptycki's armies in Byelorussia, followed by a rapid pursuit of the fleeing remnants that would take him right into Warsaw – fighting a pitched battle for the city after a six-hundred-kilometre forced march would be madness. In his reports and his later writings and lectures, he maintained that he did destroy Szeptycki's forces, and claims to have 'smashed, shattered, pulverized, completely demoralized and rendered unfit for further action' Żeligowski's two divisions no fewer than three times between the Dvina and the Bug. Those closer to the front took a more realistic view. 'During the period when the Armies of the Western Front enjoyed the most favourable numerical superiority,' writes Putna, 'they successfully carried out a series of operations in the area between the Berezina and the Bug, but they did not once manage to destroy or seriously disrupt the Polish Armed Forces acting in the same area.'[17]

Even though he had failed in the first element of his plan, Tukhachevsky was still in a strong position throughout the month of July, as his rapid advance had the effect of reducing, disrupting and demoralizing the forces opposed to him to such an extent that if he had been capable of keeping it up relentlessly he might still have been able to sweep into Warsaw on their tails. At the beginning of August he still held the initiative, and the Poles could not wrest it from him as long as he kept up the pace of his advance. But this trump card, speed, was wrenched from him by the actions of Żeligowski in the Narew basin and Sikorski on the Bug. They stopped the Russian advance in its tracks for six days, thereby giving the Poles a chance to regroup and strike back. Tukhachevsky was not seriously troubled; he did not believe the Poles capable of seizing that chance. Like Lenin, he made light of what the Bolsheviks called 'stupid patriotism', and thought Poland was defeated.

Poland was a more resilient polity and a more cohesive society than Tukhachevsky, Lenin or even most of her own allies suspected. The new threat to her continued existence so soon after the recovery of statehood galvanized large sections of society. The Catholic Church intensified pressure on the faithful to stand firm against the wiles of communism and to support the army and the government. The government and other agencies produced a barrage of propaganda, supported by lurid posters, many tinged with anti-Semitism, creating the impression of a vast alien conspiracy threatening every aspect of Polish life. And in Piłsudski the country had a leader capable of channelling the patriotic surge. While his political position had suffered as a result of his ill-judged offensive in Ukraine, he was still the commander-in-chief and exerted enormous authority.

Piłsudski had been working hard throughout the past three months to create reserves and amass supplies, and even though the supply route through Danzig had been blocked by German dockers and the others severely disrupted by strike action, he did manage to create large stockpiles at Warsaw. In mid-July he had issued a call for volunteers, which was to yield 164,615 men and women in the space of six weeks. General Haller, who was entrusted with the task of organizing them, formed some 30,000 of the men into an independent Volunteer Division, and the rest into either platoons and companies to be attached to existing units or refills to be fed into depleted units, while the women made up defence battalions based in Warsaw and other threatened towns.[18]

These volunteers represented a wide social spectrum, including members of the Polish parliament, the Sejm, teachers and civil servants, students, scouts, workers and peasants, the majority under twenty years of age. Their arrival in the ranks in the second week of August would be like an injection of fresh blood, raising morale as well as adding strength. But everything ultimately depended on how this strength was going to be applied.

General Weygand of the Inter-Allied Mission had been working on a plan to save the situation, as had the Polish Chief-of Staff, General Tadeusz Rozwadowski, an able commander with a distinguished career in the Austro-Hungarian army behind him. They had come up with broadly similar strategies. Rozwadowski was for strengthening the two wings of the Northern Front, which could then launch simultaneous counterattacks that would relieve pressure on the centre. Weygand wanted to create a strong force in the Ostrołęka–Łomża area which would stabilize the front, permitting the creation of *'une ligne forte'*, and then launch a counterattack. Neither of these plans was viable in the circumstances.[19]

With characteristic scorn, Piłsudski left them to it while he applied himself to the formulation of his own plan, without deigning to tell them that they were wasting their time. He meant to announce it on 6 August, the sixth anniversary of the day on which he had marched out at the head of his Legion in 1914. But his inward state did not reflect his outward show of confidence. 'Everything looked black and hopeless,' he wrote. He was weighed down by a sense of responsibility for having brought on disaster by his decision to strike in Ukraine first, and the fall of Brześć had deeply depressed him. At the same time he realized that only a bold plan could provide the psychological breakthrough required to make the army turn around and not only fight but win, and only he was capable of carrying it through.

On the night of 5 August Piłsudski shut himself away in a room of Warsaw's Belvedere Palace. As he pondered the various possibilities, he was reminded of Napoleon's dictum that a general working on a plan is in the same state as a woman in childbirth. But he was also keenly aware that he was a self-taught amateur. 'At times I could really hear something sneering and gibbering at me from the corners of the room as I sat there making decisions and calculations based on the absurd and the ridiculous,' he writes.[20]

Ever since the Polish retreat had passed the wedge of the Pripet, the left or southern flank of the advancing Russian front had become exposed, and this fact was exacerbated by the fact that its right wing, consisting of Gai's Konkorpus and Sergeyev's IV Army, had, by drawing ahead of the rest, elongated it. Szeptycki had tried to exploit this back in mid-July, and Piłsudski had subsequently hoped to launch a northward strike from Brześć into Tukhachesky's flank and rear. As the Russian advance continued in the same manner, with the right wing drawing further north and west, this plan became even more alluring. But with the fall of Brześć, there was no obvious place from which to launch it.

Piłsudski decided to take a major risk. Abandoning all notion of holding the line of the Bug, he would disengage his armies, pull them right back, and transfer the decisive clash to the very gates of Warsaw. He would buy time with space. Like a matador leading on a bull, he would sidestep it in order to plunge a dart in its back. He would leave a passive screen to defend the capital, and use the rest of his forces to strike upwards from the centre, across

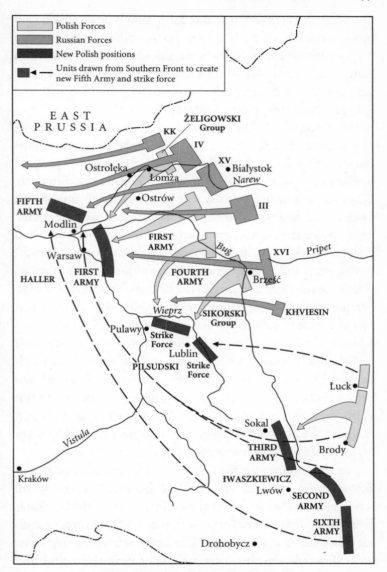

Polish Forces
Russian Forces
New Polish positions
Units drawn from Southern Front to create new Fifth Army and strike force

EAST PRUSSIA

ŻELIGOWSKI Group

KK

IV

XV • Białystok

Ostrołęka
Łomża
Narew

Ostrów

III

FIFTH ARMY

Modlin

Warsaw

FIRST ARMY

Bug

XVI Pripet

HALLER

FIRST ARMY

FOURTH ARMY

Brześć

Wieprz SIKORSKI Group

KHVIESIN

Puławy

Strike Force

Lublin

PILSUDSKI Strike Force

Łuck

Vistula

Sokal

Kraków

THIRD ARMY

Brody

IWASZKIEWICZ

Lwów • SECOND ARMY

SIXTH ARMY

Drohobycz •

The Polish Regrouping Operation

the flanks and backs of the four Russian armies closing in on their prize.

The plan was fraught with danger, as one false move could bring about the fall of the city. But at least it gave the Polish army a chance of recovering its balance. The other point to recommend this plan over Weygand's and Rozwadowski's was that while theirs envisaged a pitched battle which might or might not have destroyed the Russian armies, this one would, if it worked, yield incomparably more spectacular results.

The following morning, 6 August, Rozwadowski called at the Belvedere and helped Piłsudski work out the final dispositions. The Polish forces were reorganized entirely. The Northern Front, under General Haller, was to cover the whole area from the East Prussian border in the north down as far as Puławy on the Vistula. Its role was to defend Warsaw and tie down Tukhachevsky's forces. A new Central Front, commanded by Piłsudski himself, was to run from Puławy along the river Wieprz and down as far as Sokal. While the units defending Warsaw tied down Tukhachevsky's four armies, this was to launch a multi-pronged attack into their underbelly and sweep into their rear. The Southern Front, under General Wacław Iwaszkiewicz, was to tie down Budionny and defend Lwów and the Drohobycz oilfields. The Central Front was to launch its attack on 17 August. The plan was sound as well as daring, and having had sight of it General Weygand telegraphed Marshal Foch endorsing it fully.[21]

The regrouping process would be complex and hazardous. The Fourth Army, the southernmost of the existing Northern Front, would provide the basis of Piłsudski's strike force. It would therefore have to break away from the enemy and then make a dash southwards to the line of the river Wieprz, a lateral march along Sollohub's front during which it would be extremely vulnerable. This would provide Piłsudski with three of the five divisions he needed. For the rest he looked to Śmigły-Rydz, whose Third Army was to play a passive role in the overall plan as part of the Southern Front facing Yegorov. He picked the 1st and 3rd Legionary Divisions, his favourite units. Their withdrawal would have to be carried out with the utmost secrecy, so as not to let Yegorov know that the forces facing the Konarmia were being weakened.

The same went for Iwaszkiewicz's Southern Front, from which some hardened units such as Krajowski's 18th Division were to be withdrawn to bolster the Northern Front at Warsaw, and part of whose cavalry was to be sent north to face Gai. Given that the units had to be moved in the space of a few days, the right supplies provided for them, new staffs created and commanders installed, all under the nose of the advancing Russians, the opportunities for confusion and disaster were endless, but in the event the whole operation was carried out with remarkable expedition.

The success of the regrouping operation augured well: the matador had sidestepped the charging bull, and was in a position to deal it the death-blow. But one fundamental question remained unanswered: would the Polish troops who had fallen into the habit of retreating every day for the past six weeks and abandoning positions at the hint of enemy attack now stand and fight? Tukhachevsky might stampede the Polish army into Warsaw yet.

Curiously enough, both Piłsudski and Tukhachevsky were acting on false assumptions. Piłsudski believed that the main Russian attack would be aimed straight at the Warsaw bridgehead, where all the tanks and the heavy artillery would be waiting for it. He had even, on 8 August, amended his plan in order to strengthen this sector. But he was wrong, as Tukhachevsky had settled on a different course, on the basis of an equally false assumption.

Ever since Żeligowski's action in the Narew basin, Tukhachevsky was convinced that the latter's group represented the only remaining serious concentration of Polish forces. When Żeligowski proceeded to withdraw towards Modlin, Tukhachevsky assumed that the Poles were intending to make a stand there, on the northern approaches to Warsaw. This suited him. He assumed the eastern bridgehead of Warsaw would be an inferno of trenches and barbed wire, behind which lay the last and most serious obstacle, the river Vistula, and he wished to avoid a pitched battle in such conditions. He would rather take on the main Polish forces before Modlin, particularly as he had them outflanked already, with Gai's Konkorpus bypassing them to the north.[22]

On 8 August, two days after Piłsudski had announced his plan, Tukhachevsky issued his order for the capture of Warsaw. Gai was to move west, bypassing the capital completely, cross the Vistula and cut the Warsaw–Danzig railway. He would only be brought into the action if the Poles required extra softening up. Komand-Arm Aleksandr Shuvayev, who had taken over command of the IV Army from the wounded Sergeyev, was to follow Gai and then veer round to cross the Vistula north-west of Warsaw. Kork's XV Army was to strike at Modlin and then move south, while Lazarevich's III Army bore down on the city from the north-east. Only Sollohub's XVI Army was to attack Warsaw from the east. Khviesin's Mozyr Group, which had fallen behind in the advance, was to cover his flank. Warsaw was to be in Russian hands by 14 August.[23]

Kamenev was uneasy about Tukhachevsky's dispositions. He believed the main Polish forces were retreating not on Modlin but on Warsaw itself, and that Tukhachevsky's spearheads were therefore being directed into a void, whereas, being so far ahead, if they were to swing south they would come between the retreating Poles and Warsaw. More to the point, he had noticed that the Polish forces facing Sollohub had vanished, and suspected they were regrouping somewhere. In the course of a telegraphic conversation on 10 August he made a final attempt to convince Tukhachevsky that by shifting the whole centre of gravity of his forces north-wards he was exposing his southern flank, and should redirect Kork's and Lazarevich's armies on a more southerly course forth-with. Tukhachevsky parried by saying that his flank should be covered by the XII Army and the Konarmia, and insisted that Kamenev see to it.[24]

This was a sore point. Kamenev had issued orders to the effect that the three armies of the South-Western Front operating in Poland be transferred to Tukhachevsky's command, but these had been quietly ignored by Yegorov and Stalin. On 2 August, after discussing the matter with other members of the Politburo, Lenin telegraphed Stalin telling him the South-Western Front should concentrate on defeating the White Army of General Wrangel in the Crimea, and leave Poland to Tukhachevsky. The South-Western Front was to be divided, with its western part being joined to the Western Front and the rest going to the Southern Front.

Stalin was having none of it. Over the next two weeks he would make Yegorov ignore every order coming from Kamenev and pur-sue his own course, which lay through Lwów, southern Poland and Silesia, from where his armies would be in a position to threaten Prague, Vienna and Budapest. He sent Lenin a petulant telegram to the effect that the Politburo should keep its nose out of military matters, describing Kamenev's orders as 'nonsense', denigrating Tukhachevsky and threatening to resign his post.[25]

Stalin did have a point. With every day that passed the transfer of the three armies to Tukhachevsky's command became less fea-sible. As Tukhachevsky drew away to the north and west, not even the fast-moving Konarmia could possibly come to his aid or play a part in the forthcoming battle for Warsaw.

While both Tukhachevsky and Piłsudski had misconstrued each other's intentions, each was given an inkling of them and chose to ignore it. A day or two after issuing his own orders,

Tukhachevsky was handed a copy of Piłsudski's, found on the body of a dead Polish officer. Tukhachevsky thought it was a hoax and ignored it. He reasoned that the officer belonged to the 1st Legionary Division and had been killed in action against the 25th Chapayev Division of Voskanov's XII Army; according to the order his division should have been miles away, preparing to strike into Tukhachevsky's rear. In fact, the 1st Legionary had decided to win freedom of action for itself by lashing out at Voskanov before moving away. By the time the order was taken from the officer's body, the unit was entraining for its new concentration point.

Piłsudski, for his part, had received intelligence reports, confirmed by air reconnaissance, that a large proportion of Tukhachevsky's forces was marching west along the East Prussian frontier, bypassing the capital entirely. He assumed these to be Gai's Konkorpus and other spearheads making a deep flanking march, and did nothing about it. But both commanders remained uneasy as the moment of revelation approached. Piłsudski went so far as to write out his resignation as commander-in-chief and head of state, to be tendered if his gamble were to fail. The Polish government had received a communication from London to the effect that the Entente regarded his removal as a precondition of coming to Poland's rescue.[26]

Piłsudski was desperate to escape the oppressive atmosphere of Warsaw. Inevitably, everyone looked to him for some hint of hope, which he found hard to bear given the uncertainties gnawing away at him. 'Piłsudski's face looked terribly tired and haggard, and his eyes shone with an ominous light,' according to one witness. Haller had 'never seen him in such a state of depression and nerves'. When asked what he thought of the situation by General Carton de Wiart, Piłsudski merely shrugged his shoulders and said that it was all in the hands of the Almighty. General Weygand rather agreed. 'Your prayers can help more on this day than all our military skill,' he replied when the Papal Nuncio in Warsaw, Cardinal Achille Ratti (the future Pope Pius XI), asked him what his chances were on 14 August.[27]

On 12 August, after a final briefing with Rozwadowski and Weygand, Piłsudski left for his new headquarters at Puławy, which he reached the following day, making a detour to see his wife and daughter in the country on the way. In the circumstances, his decision to leave Warsaw and take personal command of the strike force on the river Wieprz was eccentric: he was in effect handing overall command and the responsibility of carrying through his battle-plan to Rozwadowski while he himself selected a minor, if vital, role. Although the need to ensure that the strike force was led with sufficient élan was a major factor in his decision, another was undoubtedly the fear that in Warsaw he would be subjected to the advice, opinions, arguments, reproaches and intrigues of the generals and politicians, most of whom he despised and could not trust himself to treat with civility under strain.

When he arrived at the front he was relieved to find the troops in better spirits than he had expected. Their uniforms were in a terrible state, and most of them paraded before him barefoot and resembled 'a collection of tramps'. But their morale was high, and they sang lustily as they marched. Over the next two days he reviewed every unit of the Fourth Army, and this raised morale further.[28]

On 12 August, the day Tukhachevsky had originally expected to take the city, the two armies slowly engaged outside Warsaw as Sollohub began to probe the Polish defences on the east bank of the Vistula. These were being held by a reinforced First Army, now under the command of General Franciszek Latinik, an energetic man with grand ideas on earthworks and saturation bombardment. He had been disappointed to find that there was little barbed wire available, that the sappers were inexperienced in trench-building and that the wooded terrain made accurate bombardment impossible. He nevertheless contrived to build three defensive perimeters along which he disposed 275 pieces of artillery, three armoured trains and forty tanks.[29]

On 13 August Sollohub attacked the outer perimeter in force, and the Polish 11th Division abandoned its positions and fled. Sollohub's 27th Omsk Division pursued it and was joined unexpectedly by the 21st Rifle Division of Lazarevich's army, which had strayed into the wrong sector. Together they overran the little town of Radzymin, twenty kilometres from Warsaw, but happily for the Poles the two units became so entangled that they were unable to pursue their advantage.[30]

While the loss of Radzymin was of little consequence from the tactical point of view, the news, embroidered with rumour as it travelled back, spread fear throughout Warsaw. And the behaviour of the 11th Division alarmed the front command. It was known to be suffering from low morale, and one of its regiments was overwhelmingly made up of deserters who had been caught and sent back to the ranks. But its poor showing nevertheless raised the question of how many other units might prove unable to break the habit of the past six weeks.

General Haller, whose Northern Front included Latinik's First Army and Sikorski's Fifth Army to the north of the capital, was seriously concerned. He had already decided that the best way of galvanizing the troops into a more positive mood would be to give them a more active role and to dress up the need to expel the Russians from Radzymin and close up the defensive perimeter as part of a general attack. 'Tomorrow, 14 August, we shall do battle for Warsaw, a battle for the freedom of Poland,' his orders began.[31]

While the Lithuanian-Byelorussian division was to launch an attack on the Russians at Radzymin, Sikorski's Fifth Army was to go over to the offensive further north. Haller and his staff were

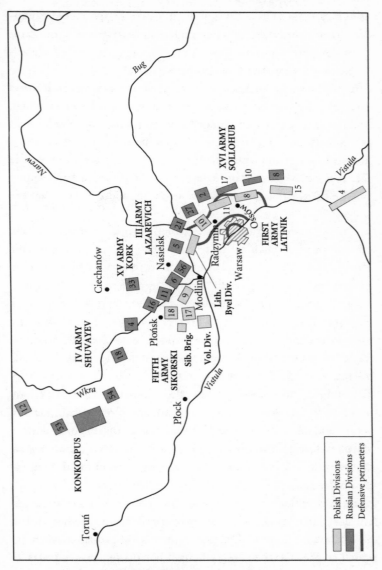

The Battle for Warsaw, 14 August

convinced that Tukhachevsky's main forces were directed at Latinik's sector, and intended to use Sikorski to relieve this. But their premises were hopelessly inaccurate.

Russian calculations of Tukhachevsky's forces at the beginning of the battle for Warsaw vary between totals of 101,269 and 132,189 front-line combatants; according to the lower estimate, 68,573 were operating in Sikorski's sector, and only 32,696 were facing Latinik. The latter, with 42,485 men, supported by heavy artillery, tanks and aircraft, was therefore relatively safe, while Sikorski would be outnumbered by over two and a half to one. But Sikorski's position was far worse than even those figures suggest.[32]

The line between the East Prussian frontier and the fortress of Modlin, laid down as his front in the order of 6 August, had already been breached by Gai's Konkorpus and other Russian units. And Sikorski's Fifth Army, supposedly 26,000 strong, existed only on paper. Krajowski's 18th Division was still on its way from Brody. The Siberian Brigade had arrived, but its equipment had gone astray. There was no sign of the 9th Division, while the 17th Poznań Division was just trudging in after its long retreat, desperate for a few days' rest. The Volunteer Division had also arrived, but Sikorski had doubts as to the military worth of these untried civilians. As his left flank had already been turned by Gai and Shuvayev, he drew up the forces at his disposal along a defensive line behind the river Wkra, with his left wing anchored on the little town of Płońsk and his right on Modlin, and hoped for the best.

He was predictably angry when he received Haller's order to attack at dawn on 14 August in order to distract the Russians from the Radzymin area, and pointed out that he had no army with which to do this: the cavalry he had been promised had finally arrived, minus its ammunition train; the Siberian Brigade was still without its rifles; the Volunteer Division's supplies were on a siding outside Kraków. After some sharp telegraphic exchanges with Haller and his chief-of-staff, during which Sikorski sarcastically explained that he could not win battles with lists of non-existent units, a compromise was reached: on the afternoon of 14 August he went into action with the forces at his disposal – Krajowski's 18th Division and the Siberian Brigade, some 8,000 men in all.[33]

Tukhachevsky could hardly contain his delight when he heard about this attack. 'For five weeks the White-Polish armies had continuously avoided any encounter with us, on account of the poor morale of their troops,' he wrote. 'It was only on the Vistula that they decided to fight, after being reinforced with fresh formations. We knew that somewhere we would come upon their main forces and smash them in a decisive engagement. And now the enemy himself was giving us the opportunity of doing just that; his Fifth Army, weakest in spirit and numbers, launched an attack on our XV and III Armies, while our freshest and most spirited units, the divisions of the IV Army, hung poised over its left flank. The Front command could hardly control its joy...'[34]

They could well afford to rejoice. Krajowski collided head-on with the main body of Kork's XV Army, while the Siberians came up against Lazarevich's formidable Petrograd Division, which flung them back across the Wkra in disorder. By nightfall, Krajowski was completely surrounded near Płońsk, and most of the Wkra as well as two of Modlin's outlying redoubts were in Russian hands.

It was not only Sikorski who was in trouble that night. Latinik had retaken Radzymin, only to lose it again a few hours later. The Lithuanian-Byelorussian Division, which had ousted the Russians, had been slow to take up defensive positions, and a vigorous Russian counterattack had not only retaken the town but broken through the second defensive perimeter. If the first fall of

Radzymin could be blamed on chance, bad luck or just the 11th Division, for the second there was no excuse. Reserves had been poured in with orders to hold on at all costs, yet they had been incapable of stopping the Russian infantry.

The Russians had also breached the perimeter further south, taking Ossów as the Polish 8th Division broke and fled. An eye-witness tells of how he saw a battalion of Polish infantry abandon its positions and run at the mere sight of Cossacks in the distance, even though the Cossacks in question turned out to be nothing more threatening than a herd of bullocks. What Sikorski called 'the hypnosis of retreat' still gripped the men.[35]

'The danger loomed before us in all its grimness as we watched more and more troops, well uniformed and armed, give way to terror, unable to utter a word and seeing their only chance in flight,' wrote Prime Minister Wincenty Witos, who toured the front line that day. 'When asked where they were running to, they looked over their shoulders in terror instead of answering.'[36]

The situation was indeed grim, and the febrile atmosphere in the city added an element of unpredictability to the military position. Russian advance units were less than twenty kilometres from Warsaw, and rumour saw Cossack patrols in the suburbs. Communist sympathizers and workers gathered expectantly, and there were a number of acts of sabotage. Haller and Rozwadowski were so worried that they telegraphed Piłsudski pressing him to go into action, and he agreed to bring forward the start of his offensive by twenty-four hours.

While most of the foreign diplomats had left, the city had filled with refugees from eastern Poland, and these contributed to the mood of suppressed panic. As it was the eve of the feast of the Assumption, churches were crammed with people praying to the Virgin for deliverance. Lord D'Abernon of the Inter-Allied Mission recorded that religious processions were so numerous he had difficulty driving across the city. Members of Piłsudski's former underground military organization were stockpiling grenades at strategic windows in preparation for a last stand in the city. Armed scouts and battalions of uniformed women patrolled the streets or manned key points. Others waited with resignation, listening to the dull thud of artillery coming from the eastern defences. Had Sollohub been able to push home his advantage that night, he might well have taken the city.[37]

When the Russian attack did resume the following morning, 15 August, it met with determined resistance. Latinik had brought in Żeligowski's 10th Division, reinforced with two companies of tanks. This stopped the Russian attack in its tracks and the Poles then retook Radzymin.

The Russians met with greater success to the north, where Kork and Lazarevich bore down on Sikorski's Fifth Army. This was in a hopeless position. Not only was it outnumbered by over two to one by these two armies, it had Shuvayev's IV Army on its flank and Gai's Konkorpus threatening its rear. Sikorski was not a man easily intimidated. Born into the impoverished minor nobility of south-eastern Poland, he had graduated as a civil engineer before turning to subversion and, in the years leading up to the Great War, to paramilitary action. He had served in the Austrian army and in the Legion, and been imprisoned like Piłsudski. At thirty-nine, he was younger than Piłsudski, but he exerted considerable authority and was much loved by his soldiers, even though he was a strict commander, demanding of others the high standards he set himself.

As he could do nothing about Shuvayev and Gai, Sikorski ignored them, and concentrated on one thing at a time, beginning with Lazarevich. He despatched an armoured company of half a dozen Fords and Fiats covered with armour plating and bristling with machine guns to distract Shuvayev, a cavalry brigade under

General Karnicki to sever communications between Shuvayev and Kork, and Krajowski's 18th Division to tie down Kork, while the rest of his forces attacked Lazarevich's III Army.

This attack soon ground to a halt and developed into a slogging match over possession of the river Wkra, but Sikorski's other dispositions yielded unexpectedly positive results. Karnicki's cavalry brigade slipped through an unoccupied piece of country between the IV and XV armies and into Shuvayev's rear. His lancers attacked supply-details and other formations, and took prisoner the entire staff of the 18th Yaroslavl Division. In the late morning they swept into Ciechanów, to which Shuvayev had moved his headquarters from Wilno on the previous day. Shuvayev himself leapt into a car with a couple of officers and managed to make his escape, but the rest of his staff, his papers, his war-chest and, most important, the IV Army's transmitter, fell into Polish hands.[38]

Kork was obliged to send in his reserve, the 33rd Kuban Division. While this had no trouble in reoccupying Ciechanów, since Karnicki had vanished as soon as he had done his worst, the diversion had checked Kork's advance, which gave Krajowski and his 18th Division a respite and allowed him to gain local advantage. By the end of the day, Sikorski, who had managed to repulse Lazarevich and even to push him back slightly from Modlin, was in a far better position and had effectively managed to surmount the crisis. Karnicki's raid on Ciechanów had bought him valuable time. And he had at last managed to deploy most of the forces placed at his disposal by Piłsudski.

An even graver crisis had been weathered that day outside Warsaw, where Sollohub's XVI Army had resumed its assault. Undeterred by the intervention of Żeligowski's 10th Division, which had reoccupied Radzymin in the morning, the Russians had gone over to the attack once more, and Radzymin had changed hands for the fifth time in two days. Latinik and his divisional commanders appeared to have lost control of the situation entirely. Haller and Rozwadowski were so alarmed that they ordered a cordon of military police to take up positions behind the front line and to machine-gun any retreating troops. These measures apparently did the trick, as observers noted a sudden change of heart and even a new self-assurance in the men who had been abandoning their positions only that morning. This would be borne out by the heavy losses in the ensuing struggle for Radzymin, which was duly retaken by the Poles that evening. Towards the end of the day a rumour began to circulate that the Virgin Mary had appeared in the heavens above the Polish lines and led them to victory. This may have had something to do with the fact that priests were noticeably to the fore, and much was made of the death of Father Ignacy Skorupka, who fell leading the attack, crucifix in hand.[39]

Vitovt Putna, whose 27th Omsk Rifle Division had once again taken Radzymin in the morning, also felt that something had changed in the afternoon of 15 August. 'The moment had come when not only individual units but the whole mass of the army suddenly lost faith in the possibility of success against the enemy,' he writes. 'It was as though a cord that we had been stretching since the Bug had suddenly snapped.'[40]

Having failed to sweep into Warsaw on the heels of a panicked Polish army or to destroy Sikorski's force and enter it from the north, Tukhachevsky had effectively lost his chance of taking the city. But this was not immediately apparent to him. Nor indeed to the inhabitants of Warsaw. The night of 15 August was the most anguished yet for the capital. The recapture of Radzymin offered little comfort, since it had been lost before. Rumours of plots and coups flew around the city as the Russian guns continued to thud at the defences and, within, communist agitators set warehouses ablaze. And if the next day was relatively quiet on the Warsaw bridgehead, it was anything but for Sikorski, whose Fifth Army was to be tested to the limit.

Although he had survived the crisis of 15 August relatively well, Sikorski was still in a desperate position. His front line was thinly stretched along the river Wkra, on the other side of which were two Russian armies bent on destroying him. A third, Shuvayev's IV, was hovering over his left flank, and Polish intelligence had intercepted an order from him instructing it to fall on that flank at Płońsk: that very morning, Tukhachevsky had issued fresh orders setting the destruction of the Polish Fifth Army as a priority.[41]

During a conference attended by Weygand, Sosnkowski and Rozwadowski, General Haller tried to persuade Sikorski to cut his losses, abandon the line of the Wkra and fall back on that of the Vistula, effectively wheeling his front line to an east–west axis and covering his rear. Sikorski argued that there was nothing particularly safe about the positions they were proposing, and that abandoning the Wkra, which his troops had fought over so doggedly, would be bad for morale. By withdrawing, he would be inviting the eventual combined attack of all three Russian armies, which was what he had been hoping to avoid. He calculated that he should be able to repulse Lazarevich's III Army that day, before the other two could bring their full force to bear, and that he would then be in a position to deal with them on the morrow. Haller gave his assent.[42]

The all-out attack Sikorski launched on the morning of 16 August proved too weak to break the Russian lines. Lazarevich and Kork were two days behind schedule, and desperate to drive home their attack on Modlin. The fight put up by the Petrograd Division in particular demonstrated that, unlike Sollohub's, these troops still had every intention of reaching their goal. Despite the use of armoured trains to support their attack, the Poles could make no headway against them.

Meanwhile, further to the north, Kork moved against Krajowski's 18th Division, spread over a large area between Nasielsk and Ciechanów. His Kuban Division, reinforced by a couple of regiments of Cossacks, swooped on one of its battalions and annihilated it. As the Cossacks pursued the fleeing remnants they penetrated deep into Krajowski's grouping, and only the old general's quick reaction prevented his division being sliced in half. But hardly had this crisis been contained than a new one began to develop, on Sikorski's left wing.

Long before he had expected any threat from that quarter, the 18th Yaroslavl Division of Shuvayev's IV Army turned up outside the little town of Płońsk, defended only by a battalion of sailors and some volunteers from Pomerania. As soon as he heard the news, Sikorski drove over, but by the time he arrived Russian infantry was pouring into the town, which contained Krajowski's supply-train. It looked as though the fate of that division and of the entire Fifth Army was sealed. But at that critical moment, a reinforcement promised to Sikorski some time before, the 1st Light Horse Regiment, appeared on the scene.

'As the church towers of Płońsk came in sight, we heard the rattle of machine guns and the sound of a fight raging in the town,' wrote one of its troopers. 'We could see individual soldiers running away. There was not a moment to lose…One loud word of command, and like a hurricane the whole regiment galloped into the broad street leading to the market square, scattering the fleeing soldiers. The square itself was so cluttered with carts that it was difficult to get through. At the end of the street leading into it from the west we could see the last of the retreating defenders, and just behind them the long gleaming bayonets of the Russian infantry…Then, drawing sabres, the whole regiment surged forward, led by its commander. We charged into the throng, carrying everything before us like a whirlwind and sweeping out the unsuspecting enemy.'[43]

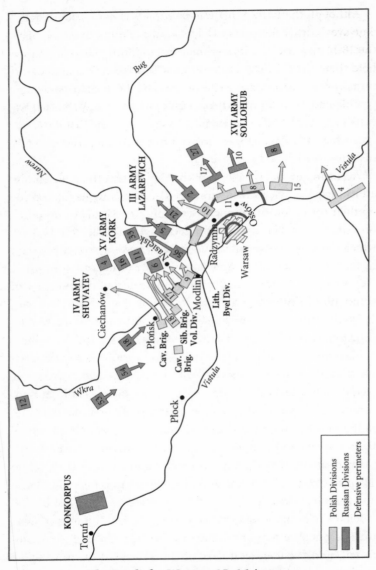

The Battle for Warsaw, 15–16 August

Although the Fifth Army was saved, it was not out of danger. Shuvayev's other divisions would soon be coming up to support the 18th, and one cavalry regiment could hardly be expected to hold them back. Unless he could finish off Lazarevich soon and transfer some of his forces to the defence of Płońsk, Sikorski would be obliged to call off his attack and follow the plan suggested by Haller and Weygand of falling back to the line of the Vistula – and executing such a manoeuvre under pressure might prove fatal for his army.

Accordingly, he issued fresh orders to the three divisions attacking Lazarevich's III Army at Nasielsk, urging them to speed up their operation. He threw in the Siberian Brigade in support, bringing the total number of infantry attacking Nasielsk to 14,500, which more or less evened the odds. The town was to be occupied by four o'clock that afternoon 'without fail and regardless of cost'. He threatened shirkers and officers who dragged their feet with summary justice.[44]

'As we drove in the direction of Nasielsk we passed numerous detachments hurrying into battle,' records Prime Minister Witos. 'Only a small number of the soldiers had complete uniforms, and those were in tatters. At least half of them had no boots; their feet bled as they marched over the sharp stubble-fields. Many had no tunics at all, with only the remains of shirts and breeches clinging to their bodies. But they all carried rifles and ammunition, while their talk showed confidence and faith in victory. Some complained that they had marched barefoot all the way from Kiev. Their feet resembled pieces of scorched leather, covered in blood and festering sores.'[45]

Fierce fighting developed as the three Polish divisions moved in. The pressure brought to bear by the Siberian Brigade began to tell, and the counterattacks of the Petrograd Division grew weaker. Gradually, it started to give ground, as did its companions, the 5th and 6th. As their ammunition ran out, the Petrograd Division, composed almost entirely of Bolsheviks, tried to halt the Polish advance with bayonet charges, but they could not keep this up for long, and at a couple of minutes to four o'clock General Osiński marched into Nasielsk at the head of the 9th Division, closely followed by the 17th Poznań Division, the Volunteer Division and the Siberian Brigade, each entering from a different side. Lazarevich's men fell back on Serock and Pułtusk, and Sikorski was able to wheel round to face Kork and Shuvayev.

'It seemed as though the fate of the enemy's Fifth Army had been settled,' Tukhachevsky later wrote. 'Its destruction would have had a decisive effect on all further operations. But the Poles were lucky. Their Fifth Army was saved. With complete impunity, despite the presence on its flanks of four divisions of riflemen and two of Cossacks, it continued to attack our XV and III Armies. This simply unthinkable and monstrous situation helped the Poles not only to halt the advance of these two armies, but also to push them back step by step whence they had come.'[46]

Although luck did play an important part in the fighting along the Wkra, it would have availed Sikorski little had Tukhachevsky been fully in control of his forces. The Fifth Army was within his grasp for two whole days, but he had failed to clasp it. Sikorski, whose role in the battle of Warsaw was never intended to be a leading one, had mesmerized and held Tukhachevsky's main forces, thereby making it possible for Piłsudski's plan to work even though it had been based on a false premise.

Piłsudski had been monitoring events at Warsaw from his headquarters in Puławy, glad to be far from what he called 'the pontificating cowardice and theorizing helplessness' of his entourage in the capital. But he grew alarmed when reports reached him of the fall of Radzymin and the poor showing of the troops defending Warsaw. He had dedicated what he considered to be

General Śmigły-Rydz greeting the Ukrainian leader Ataman Symon Petlura and his government at the railway station in Kiev, May 1920.

Recruits of the Ukrainian National Army parade before Petlura, May 1920.

Above Vladimir Ilych Lenin calling for volunteers to fight Poland, May 1920. On the steps of the platform stands Lev Davidovich Trotsky, the creator of the Red Army.

Right Mikhail Nikolaevich Tukhachevsky, the twenty-seven-year-old commander of the army which was to invade Poland and carry revolution into Europe.

Below General Stanislaw Szeptycki, commander of the Polish Northern Front. He had achieved the rank of general in the Austro-Hungarian army and commanded the Polish Legion during the First World War, but realised the coming conflict would be a challenge of a new kind.

Above Joseph Stalin, political officer to the Russian South-Western Front, had his own ideas on how to conduct the campaign, and contributed to its failure by his insubordination.

Above right Aleksandr Yegorov, who had attained the rank of colonel in the Imperial Russian Army despite his peasant origins, commanded the South-Western Front, but was little more than Stalin's executive.

Right Semion Mikhailovich Budionny (standing), flamboyant commander of the Russian First Cavalry Army, the Konarmia, with his political commissar, Klimentii Efreimovich (Klim) Voroshilov; two of Stalin's closest acolytes.

Right Gai (Gaia Dmitrievich Bzhishkian), the Armenian-born commander of the Russian 3rd Cavalry Corps, KonKorpus III, which spearheaded the Russian advance with panache and marked its retreat with savagery.

Below These soldiers of Budionny's Konarmia might be studying a bulletin entitled 'To Victory!', but by the time this photograph was taken, in July 1920, the Konarmia was under severe strain. Note the liberal attitude to uniform and the typical Russian footwear, confected from strips of birch-bark and pieces of old tyre.

Below Units of the Polish First Army in retreat, early August 1920, when it looked as though the Polish forces might disintegrate.

The PolRevKom, Lenin's government for Poland. Seated in the middle are the dreaded founder of the Bolshevik political police (Cheka) Feliks Dzierżyński, the old Polish communist Julian Marchlewski and the veteran Bolshevik Feliks Kon.

Officers of the French military mission to Poland trying to make sense of the developments. Second from left, General Leonard Skierski, commander of the Fourth Army, explains the situation to General Maxime Weygand, while on the far right Major Charles de Gaulle makes his own assessment.

Above left General Józef Haller, one-time legionary officer and subsequently founder of the Polish 'Blue Army' in France, took charge of the volunteers coming forward in defence of Poland, and assumed command of the Northern Front in the critical days of the battle for Warsaw.

Above General Wacław Iwaszkiewicz took command of the Polish Southern Front and defended the city of Lwów against the Konarmia.

Left A detachment of the Women's Volunteer Legion, formed up as a last line of defence, August 1920.

Above General Władysław Sikorski, commander of the Polish Fifth Army which held the northern approaches to Warsaw, briefing a company commander on 13 August.

Right Polish machine-gun emplacement outside Warsaw, August 1920. The men are equipped with a captured Russian Maxim gun.

Below Polish Renault tanks in action at Mińsk Mazowiecki in August 1920.

Above Polish infantry of the 14th Division advancing against the flank of the Russians outside Warsaw.

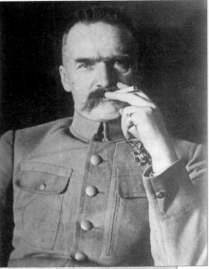

Right Józef Piłsudski, the architect and the inspiration of victory.

Below Men of Gai's KonKorpus being disarmed by German lancers as they cross the border into East Prussia in order to escape capture by the Poles.

more than enough troops to the defence of the capital, and the fact that even such numbers could not hold the line suggested either that the Polish army was disintegrating, or that the Russians had greater forces at their disposal than he had thought. Reluctantly, he agreed to bring forward his own attack by a day, in order to relieve pressure on the Warsaw defences.

Early on the morning of 16 August, as Sikorski battled with Lazarevich for possession of Nasielsk and Latinik patched up his defensive perimeter, Piłsudski launched his five divisions across the river Wieprz. The Fourth Army, which he led personally, consisted of three: General Konarzewski's 14th Poznań, Colonel Ladoś's 16th Pomeranian and General Galica's 21st Highland Divisions, with a combined strength of 27,500 infantry, 950 cavalry, 461 machine guns and ninety field guns. To their right another force, under Śmigły-Rydz, consisting of the 1st and 3rd Legionary Divisions and Jaworski's cavalry (25,000 infantry, 2,850 cavalry, 566 machine guns and 162 field guns in all), started out in a northeasterly direction. The two groups were to sweep the whole area between the perimeter of the Warsaw defences in the west and a line running from Chełm through Brześć and Białystok. Each division was to act independently, taking no notice of what might be happening on its flanks or rear, and moving forward with all possible speed. Piłsudski was thrusting a pitchfork into the Russian armies from the side: provided the thrust was sufficiently powerful, panic and chaos would preclude their rallying, and if he did not pause he could destroy them. By inverting the strategic situation, he would make all the factors which had worked for Tukhachevsky now work for him.[47]

He expected to come up against Khviesin's Mozyr Group on the first day, and the main forces of Sollohub's XVI Army on the second. He was in the dark as to Khviesin's strength, as estimates varied between 5,000 and 25,000 men (in fact, it could muster no

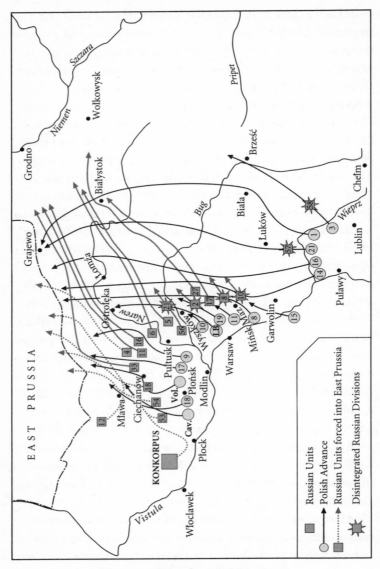

The counterstroke, 16–22 August

more than 11,690), and this made him nervous. The last thing he wanted was to have to fight a battle at the outset, as this would slow down his offensive before it had built up momentum, and would also give notice to the other Russian armies. And his unease grew throughout the first day.[48]

Galica's Highlanders encountered and defeated what looked like a detachment of Khviesin's 57th Division at Kock, and the 3rd Legionary scattered an unimpressive one belonging to the 58th, but apart from that no contact was made with the enemy. The whole Polish Central Front had advanced between thirty and fifty kilometres into an area where they had expected to find Tukhachevsky's left wing, and encountered only the odd foraging party. Piłsudski's left wing, the 14th Poznań Division, was nearing the southern perimeter of the Warsaw defences, which were reportedly under heavy attack, but the men could see and hear nothing. Piłsudski was mystified. He had to envisage the possibility that the Russians had reacted to his attack by folding back their left wing in order to create an east–west line of defence against his strike force. He therefore telegraphed Rozwadowski that evening with orders for Latinik's First Army to deliver a strong attack on Sollohub.

The following day, 17 August, brought no clarification. Piłsudski's divisions forged ahead, with the 14th passing Garwolin, the Highlanders reaching Łuków and the 1st Legionary Biała. 'Had I been dreaming not so long before, when I could feel some terrible force overwhelming me with its incessant motion, its monstrous claws reaching out for my throat?' he wrote. 'Or was I dreaming now that five divisions were merrily marching unopposed over the same area they were so recently abandoning to the enemy in the deadly terror of the retreat? This was a happy dream, but could it be real? Gripped by these dark thoughts, I reached Garwolin that evening [17 August]. I can remember as though it were yesterday that moment when I was drinking my tea and pre-paring for bed. Suddenly, I leapt to my feet; at last I heard a sound of life, a sound of reality, the sound of guns coming somewhere from the north. So the enemy was there after all!...Having lain down to sleep, I raised my head from the pillow several times just to make sure. The dull thud of artillery was calmly, slowly and regularly shaking the night, telling of a battle being fought to a steady tempo. Somewhere near Kołbiel, or maybe a little further, my 14th Division was fighting in the night.[49]

Before he did lie down to sleep he reorganized his forces, add-ing the 21st Highland Division to Śmigły-Rydz's Second Army and transferring the 15th from the defence of Warsaw to his own Fourth Army, which would strengthen the forces moving north into the Russian rear.

In the course of the following day, the three divisions of Piłsudski's Fourth Army made contact with Sollohub's XVI Army. And as they struck its flank, Żeligowski's 10th and Jung's 15th Poznań Divisions moved out of the Warsaw perimeter to attack it from the front. Sollohub's force suddenly found itself caught between two fires, and the effect was shattering. Its three southernmost divisions scattered and began a headlong retreat eastwards, only to find themselves colliding head-on with the successive prongs of Piłsudski's force.

Putna, who had been tidying up his 27th Omsk Division after its five-day struggle over Radzymin, became aware late on 17 August that something was wrong. There was no hard informa-tion, just rumour and a suspicious number of deserters from other units sneaking by in a north-easterly direction. He tried to make contact with Sollohub, without success. Early the next morning, KomDiv Kakurin of the 10th Division turned up accompanied by the commander of the 2nd Priamurskaya Division and confirmed Putna's worst fears. The 8th and 10th Divisions had ceased to exist as cohesive units, and the commander of the former had been killed in a raid by Polish lancers. The Priamurskaya was badly battered, and there was no news at all of the 17th Division. Of the five divisions making up Sollohub's force only Putna's 27th had survived. Its commander described the XVI Army's condition by the end of 18 August as 'simply catastrophic'.[50]

Earlier that day, having seen his offensive strike home, Piłsudski handed over command of the Fourth Army to General Skierski and returned to Warsaw. He knew his plan had worked and that he now had Tukhachevsky by the throat. He was determined to strangle. If he did not follow through his advantage with energy the Russian armies would simply scuttle back, re-form and launch a fresh offensive.

On his return to the capital, he found most people unaware of the dramatic shift that had taken place and fearful that Gai, who had crossed the Vistula and cut the Warsaw–Danzig railway, might sweep into Warsaw from the undefended west. One of the few who had taken in the situation was Major De Gaulle. 'Ah, what a fine manoeuvre we have here!' he noted in his diary on 17 August. 'Our Poles have grown wings. The soldiers who were physically and morally exhausted only a week ago are now racing forward in leaps of 40 kilometres a day. Yes, it is Victory! Complete, triumphant Victory!'[51]

This was certainly not apparent to Tukhachevsky, who had moved his headquarters forward to Minsk, still confident that Warsaw would be his within the next four or five days. The Soviet leadership was already making further plans contingent on that. On 15 August the PolRevKom moved to the small town of Wyszków to be ready to enter Warsaw with the Red Army and take power. Moscow Radio began broadcasting appeals addressed to the soldiers of the Polish army, bristling with phrases such as 'We are your brothers in labour. With you we want to crush and destroy

your Lords,' and inciting them to form soldiers' soviets as the Bolsheviks had done in 1917. And while peace negotiations between
Russia and Poland did finally open at Minsk on 17 August, Lenin
instructed the Soviet negotiators to stall, insisting that it was
'arch-important to finish off Poland'. At a meeting on 10 August,
the Politburo had passed a resolution to send all German communists in Russia to the armies of the Western Front, and four days
later Trotsky had instructed the Comintern to compose leaflets
in German for distribution by the Red Army when it crossed the
border into Germany.[52]

One of the reasons Tukhachevsky was so out of touch was
that from the moment Piłsudski launched his offensive, the Polish radio-monitoring services switched from listening in to the
Russian radio network and began jamming it. Another was that
he was confident in his original assessment of the situation. When,
late on the evening of 17 August, he received the first reports of
a Polish offensive from the river Wieprz, he did not immediately
make the connection with the order found on the dead officer. He
persisted in his view that he was pinning the main Polish forces
down around Modlin, and took the new Polish offensive to be
no more than a diversion. He ordered Sollohub to bend back his
southern wing and create a line of defence between Radzymin
and Brześć which would prevent any Polish force from penetrating into the rear of the Russian armies. He was authorized to draw
reserves from the 60,000 equipped refills waiting at bases near
Grodno to fill out his ranks.[53]

The appropriate orders were issued by Sollohub early on 19
August, by which time contact with all his units had been lost,
and they were never received by anyone. He himself was nearly
captured by Jaworski's cavalry when it stumbled on the XVI Army
headquarters at Ostrożany in the early hours of 20 August. It was
only then he fully grasped that not only his southern wing but his

entire army had fled across the Bug. Only Putna was still holding a couple of crossings, in order to let stragglers through. The other elements of the XVI Army were streaming back towards Białystok in disorder. But having taken in the scale of the disaster, Sollohub was in no position to pass the intelligence on to the Front command.[54]

Tukhachevsky had now lost contact with both of his wings, while his centre, the XV and III Armies of Kork and Lazarevich, was being driven back by increasingly aggressive blows from Latinik and Sikorski. Yet Lenin, who was desperate that the peace talks should not reach a conclusion while Warsaw was still in Polish hands, was insisting that he make a supreme effort to take the Polish capital. Lenin also urged the PolRevKom to broadcast generous promises of land to all Polish peasants who would support the Red Army in crushing their 'Lords'.[55]

Tukhachevsky now decided to pull all his forces together into a tight phalanx. Gai and Shuvayev were to fall back on Mława and Ciechanów, whence, having been joined by Kork and Lazarevich, they could mount an all-out assault on Warsaw. At the same time he sent stern telegrams to Budionny, ordering him to make with all speed for Zamość and Lublin, in order to threaten and check whatever Polish force it was that had dealt Sollohub such a blow.[56]

Kamenev disapproved of this plan as strongly as he had of Tukhachevsky's insistence on sending Gai and Shuvayev so far ahead and shifting his whole front to the north in the first place. Given the present situation, he argued, they should squeeze out of it the only advantage it gave them: Gai and Shuvayev should be instructed to attack Warsaw from the west regardless of the critical position of the other armies. If they moved fast, he argued, they could be riding into the city from the undefended side within a couple of days. He accepted that this would leave Sollohub,

Lazarevich and Kork isolated, but argued that if Warsaw fell 'we will have won the whole war'. This was absurd, since even if Gai and Shuvayev did manage to take the city, they would be in no position to hold on to it for more than a day or two, cut off as they would be from the rest of the Russian army. But Kamenev was in Moscow, and like Lenin's, his thinking was driven by political rather than military considerations.[57]

Tukhachevsky was more inclined to leave the city to itself for the time being and seek a dénouement through a fresh confrontation with Piłsudski's forces. He sketched out a plan to reassemble all his forces along an east–west curve running from Ostrołęka through Ciechanów to Mława, from which he would strike southwards at Sikorski and at the forces advancing from the south, which, he calculated, would have begun to run out of steam by then. They would also be threatened in the rear by Budionny, who would be marching on Lublin. It might have looked promising on paper, but it was fantasy. The situation had changed so far and was continuing to change so fast that all his calculations were hopelessly out of date. His orders, which succeeded each other with astonishing prodigality, were stillborn. His forces were not where he thought they were, and the few he did manage to make contact with were in no position to carry out his designs. And he had no clear idea of where the Polish forces were or what they were doing.[58]

Far from running out of speed, the five divisions of Piłsudski's strike force were racing ahead. 'The music of war was no longer drooling out some half-hearted *contredanse*,' he recalled, 'it had switched to a lusty gallop.' The 1st Legionary Infantry Regiment had covered fifty-four kilometres on 16 August, and slept for only three hours before setting off on its second lap of thirty-seven kilometres, followed by five hours' sleep, a third lap of forty-five kilometres followed by seven hours of fighting and four of sleep, and then a four-day slog of 125 kilometres punctuated with snatches of rest, followed by a fourteen-hour battle for Białystok. In the course of thirteen days the regiment would have covered 450 kilometres and taken 12,670 prisoners and sixty guns at a total cost of under 250 dead and wounded. As De Gaulle noted admiringly, 'the Polish soldier is a marcher of extraordinary endurance'.[59]

A couple of days after the start of the strike from the Wieprz, the impetus had set all the other units of the Polish Central and Northern Fronts in motion, and by 20 August all forces in the area were moving north, the individual divisions racing each other to trap the disorientated Russian armies. By then Tukhachevsky had issued his latest and only sensible order: that of a general retreat.

Kork, whose army was still in relatively good shape, was able to conduct a fighting withdrawal, and on 21 August his 15th Division put up a spirited defence of Łomża against Skierski's Fourth Army. Lazarevich also began his retreat in good order. But since he was continually veering northwards in order to avoid the oncoming Polish spearheads, his units soon became mixed together. While this reduced their operational ability, they would be no easier for the Poles to stop than a herd of buffalo.

And even if the Russians were in full retreat, they fought with desperation to break out when cornered. Exasperation at the turn events had taken also added an edge to their treatment of prisoners. Their commissars had been deflecting the soldiers' sense of grievance at being robbed of victory and at the conditions they were forced to endure onto the Polish 'Lords'; even those fleeing for their lives in small units found time to visit elaborate tortures on any Polish officer unlucky enough to have stumbled into their path. This inevitably provoked retaliation, and the level of brutality rose considerably on both sides.

As Lazarevich's and Kork's armies moved eastward, they pulled away from Shuvayev's IV Army and Gai's Konkorpus, leaving these vulnerable to being cut off by Sikorski. Gai had reached the Vistula near Włocławek and sent detachments across in boats. They managed to capture some barges carrying military supplies from Danzig to Warsaw by shelling them from the bank and forcing them to run aground. They also wrought havoc in the area. In the absence of precise instructions from Tukhachevsky, Gai turned south and attacked Płock. The little town was defended by an assortment of military units and civilian volunteers manning hastily erected barricades, who were no match for Gai's horsemen. They fought their way into the picturesque Renaissance town and began to pillage, rape and murder on a spectacular scale. It was not until halfway through the following day, 19 August, that they were forced out by Polish detachments rushed over from Warsaw.[60]

It was only on 20 August that Gai heard of the Polish offensive and the Russian retreat, and realized that he was on his own. He promptly took command of all Shuvayev's infantry in the area and made a dash for Mława.

Two days earlier, Sikorski had issued orders aimed at intercepting him. As a result, Krajowski's 18th Division was waiting, stretched along the Ciechanów–Mława railway line, which was being patrolled by Polish armoured trains, and Sikorski's new cavalry division, under General Gustaw Orlicz-Dreszer, was on its way from Płońsk to intercept him. But persistent low-lying cloud prevented the Polish air force from locating the exact position of the Konkorpus, so all Sikorski could do was spread his forces out in a thin line in the hope of catching it. Gai moved fast, and although Orlicz-Dreszer did manage to make contact with him briefly, he had moved on before the Poles could deploy and engage him. In the early hours of 22 August, long before anyone expected, he reached the Ciechanów–Mława railway line.

Using the morning mist as cover, Gai drew up his entire force, now down to 5,000 men, into a tight formation and deployed his artillery against a short section of the track, where a battalion of Krajowski's infantry and a company of tanks lay in wait. They were taken aback by the withering barrage of fire directed at them at close quarters out of the mist, which knocked out the tanks. Gai's Cossacks then hacked their way through the Polish infantry, and rode on, followed by the remnants of Shuvayev's riflemen. The next day Gai pounced on an unsuspecting battalion of the Siberian Brigade, slaughtering some four hundred men who had surrendered, battered his way through the 13th Wilno Lancers, which attempted to halt him, and kept going. But on 24 August he came up against the 14th Poznań Division of Piłsudski's strike force, which had just reached the East Prussian border and blocked his way. The remainder of Shuvayev's men gave up and crossed the border into Germany, where they were interned. But Gai decided to make a last attempt to break through. 'Konkorpus III reached Kolno after heavy fighting,' he cabled Tukhachevsky. 'Entire infantry of IV Army crossed frontier. Will try to cut through to Grajewo. No artillery shells or ammunition left. Much loot. Please radio position of new Front.'[61]

The next day he hurled the whole Konkorpus at the Poles, but his exhausted horsemen could not hope to cut through the ranks of the Poznanian infantry. He was determined not to surrender to them, mindful of the incriminating trail of slaughter he had left behind him, so he wheeled left and crossed the border into East Prussia, where his men, still singing 'The Internationale', were disarmed and arrested by German troops.

In the fifty days since the start of Tukhachevsky's offensive, the Konkorpus had covered over eight hundred kilometres and led the advance. It had taken thousands of prisoners, terrorized the Poles and spared the main Russian forces many a battle. Its loss was not only a personal blow to Tukhachevsky, but also something in the nature of a castration for the Western Front.

At the time, Tukhachevsky had plenty of other things to worry about. The remains of the XVI Army were fleeing eastwards in small groups, often avoiding roads and towns, with only Putna's 27th Division, down to a quarter of its original strength, still a functioning unit. Putna was now both the rearguard and the left wing of the whole Western Front: having made freak radio contact with Tukhachevsky on 21 August, he had been ordered to do what he could to cover the retreat of the remnants of Sollohub's other divisions and of Khviesin's Mozyr Group.

On 22 August, as Putna approached Białystok he found a disorderly column of unarmed men from Sollohub's and Khviesin's defeated units tailing back as far as twelve kilometres. The Polish 1st Legionary Division had taken the town that morning, cutting off their retreat. Putna launched an attack which opened the road for long enough to let some of the stragglers through, but when it was closed by a counterattack from the Poles, he changed course and moved on, leaving them to their fate. On 25 August he crossed the river Niemen and made for Wołkowysk, out of reach of the right arm of the Polish strike force.[62]

The retreat of Lazarevich's III Army, which had been in far better shape than Sollohub's when it began its withdrawal, had also turned into flight, and much the same was true of Kork's XV Army. Its retreat had been orderly until it found itself caught between two Polish divisions striking at right angles across its course. It split into two, and every subsequent attempt to rally would be undone by further blows from the side. Therein lay the beauty of Piłsudski's plan.

As the prongs of his offensive thrust into the Russian columns at right angles, these had to run the gauntlet four times before they were clear. And every time one of these units found another

Polish force cutting into its flank, it would swerve northwards to avoid the blow; the consequence was a series of massive bottlenecks of troops and supply-trains outside towns such as Białystok and Grajewo, at bridges, crossing points and road junctions, resulting in mounting chaos and further disorganization of the army.

It was a rout. 'We retreated from the Vistula in complete chaos,' records Putna, 'while the army commanders stared in amazement, completely failing to take in the situation, having, as the operational documents testify, lost control of even their staffs.' Tukhachevsky's front disintegrated entirely as the instinct of self-preservation took over. According to Putna, 'the catastrophe assumed proportions even more grandiose than the Poles could possibly have hoped for'.[63]

5

Settling the Scores

ON 25 AUGUST Piłsudski's offensive came to an end as his divisions reached the East Prussian frontier. And as the last of Tukhachevsky's surviving units limped across the Niemen, the Poles began counting up the score. The haul after ten days' fighting was 50,000 prisoners (66,000 according to Soviet sources), 231 guns and 1,023 machine guns. The Red Army had lost a further 25,000 killed and at least 30,000 (and possibly as many as 80,000) interned in East Prussia, along with their arms and equipment. And while most battles have the effect of tearing more or less flesh from the bodies of the defeated units, this one had removed entire units, skeletons and all.[1]

The Konkorpus had been eliminated completely, along with its equipment, staff and commander (and a great deal of booty looted along the way). All four of Shuvayev's divisions, the 12th, 18th Yaroslavl, 53rd and 54th, had also ended up in East Prussia. All that was left of the once-powerful army was its commander, part of his staff, and two regiments which had remained in Wilno. Kork's 4th and about seven-eighths of his renowned 33rd Kuban Division had likewise crossed the German frontier. That added up to eight out of the twenty-one divisions Tukhachevsky had led into Poland two months earlier.

Of the thirteen divisions that did manage to withdraw across the Niemen, only seven were remotely fit for service. Tukhachevsky had lost over 100,000 men, and although there were plenty more where those had come from, he would have difficulty in replacing the officers who made up a high proportion of those losses. He had lost more than a battle. Like his hero Napoleon in 1812, he had lost an army.

But he refused to admit failure, to himself or anyone else. Anxious to forestall any criticism of his conduct of the campaign, he hastened to assure his superiors that the 'temporary setback' he had suffered on the Vistula was of little consequence. At the same time he began casting about for excuses. He complained about the poor condition of the armies he had been given and about alleged supply shortages, and went on to blame bad luck and, finally, Budionny, Yegorov and Stalin for not having brought the Konarmia into play. This was an irrelevance, but since he brought it up, it has to be addressed.

Just as the two fronts passed the wedge of the Pripet, drew level and made contact at the end of July, military imperatives pulled them apart. With the Konarmia blooded by the heavy fighting at Brody, Yegorov had to pause and rest. Tukhachevsky on the other hand felt obliged to quicken his pace so as not to allow the retreating Poles any respite, and veered north in pursuit of what he thought were the main Polish forces. His demands that the three armies of the South-Western Front operating in Poland be transferred to his command did not, therefore, amount to an attempt at integrating them with the rest of his forces and bringing them into play in the Warsaw operation.

Meanwhile, Yegorov had, on 6 August, received fresh orders from Kamenev instructing him to pull back the Konarmia and prepare to redirect it towards Lublin, but he later claimed that only the first part of the orders had come through, and persisted in his intention of using his force against Lwów.[2]

Two days later, on 8 August, Tukhachevsky issued his final order for the battle for Warsaw, which made no mention of the

Konarmia: he was not counting on that or on either of Yegorov's other armies, which he knew to be too far away. It was only a full week later, on 15 August, that he would order the Konarmia to move on Lublin, by which time it was far too late for it to be brought to bear in the operations around Warsaw. There is therefore no likelihood that Tukhachevsky ever intended it or any other of Yegorov's units to play a part.[3]

But if Yegorov and Stalin cannot be blamed for failing to save the day at Warsaw, they do stand accused of insubordination on a breathtaking scale. Yegorov claimed never to have received Kamenev's order of 10 August transferring command of the Konarmia and the XII and XIV Armies to Tukhachevsky's front, to take effect at midday on 14 August, and ignored the follow-up order of 12 August to the same effect. While Kamenev was dictating this second order in Moscow on the morning of 12 August, Yegorov and Stalin issued their own. 'In the absence of any orders from above', they instructed Budionny to take the field and capture Lwów. By the time Kamenev's order reached Yegorov at his headquarters in Kiev, the Konarmia was heavily engaged against Polish infantry outside Brody. Stalin was all indignation. He regarded Kamenev's order as 'needlessly frustrating', and refused to pass it on to Budionny, claiming, rightly, that it should have been issued three days earlier (which it originally was) or a week later. It was his deputy Berzin who eventually countersigned the order and sent it on to Budionny. As the order placed the Konarmia under Tukhachevsky's command but did not contain any instructions as to its immediate movements, Budionny, who received it on 14 August, battled on towards Lwów.[4]

His progress was slow. After two days' heavy fighting he reached the river Bug at Kamionka Strumiłowa, but every time he moved forward the Poles would repulse him. He was nearly captured when they raided Łopatyn in the middle of the night, and only just managed to shoot his way out. On 15 August he crossed the Bug and thrust at Lwów, but he was pushed back to the river the following day. It was at this point that he received his first specific instructions from Tukhachevsky, which were that he should disengage immediately, fall back on Włodzimierz Wołyński to regroup, and then set out for Zamość and Lublin.

Budionny had no intention of complying. The order bore only Tukhachevsky's signature and was not countersigned by the Western Front's political officer, which allowed him to query it. The following day, 17 August, he notified Tukhachevsky that he was unable to disengage immediately as, in the absence of any other unit on hand to take his place, he would be leaving a dangerous gap in the front. He suggested that the most sensible thing for him to do was to beat the Poles and capture Lwów and then march north. He was now gaining ground steadily and expected the city to be in his hands within a day or two.[5]

But on that very afternoon he had his first inkling of how long it might take. His men had to hack their way through battalions of armed schoolboys near the village of Zadworze, and as they approached the city they came across more and more volunteer units of determined citizens. Lwów was a proud bastion of Polish influence and aspiration in the east, the 'queen of the marches', and its inhabitants were building barricades, manufacturing grenades and preparing for a determined defence.

The military resistance had also stiffened, as General Iwasz-kiewicz, the commander of the Southern Front, pulled every spare unit out of other sectors. A tough soldier born in Siberia to parents who had been exiled for their part in the Insurrection of 1863, Iwaszkiewicz toured the positions armed with a bottle of vodka and a stick – the one to keep up his own spirits and the other to keep up that of his troops. The air force joined in, strafing Budionny's Cossacks as they deployed for attack, and the Polish

2nd Cavalry Division harassed them from the north. Sawicki had been replaced by the younger and more adventurous Colonel Juliusz Rómmel, a former Tsarist guards officer, who knew how to get the best out of the Polish cavalry.[6]

On 18 August Budionny drew his forces into a tight formation for a final assault on the city, which he expected to take the following day. He ignored a second order from Tukhachevsky, repeating his previous instructions. But on the next day, 19 August, his advance units were still twelve kilometres from the city, and the prospect of an easy prize was fading. A third order from Tukhachevsky, along with a telegram from Trotsky to Voroshilov insisting he cooperate with Western Front Command, could not be ignored.[7]

Budionny was seriously concerned by the morale of his men as he disengaged and marched them back across the Bug to Sokal. They had fought hard for the last seven days, and their reward had at last come in sight when they identified the spires of Lwów in the distance, only for them to be pulled out. As he had no idea about what was going on elsewhere along the front, he could not explain the situation to them; his own guess was that it was not good.[8]

At Sokal, the Konarmia joined up with the XII Army, now under KomandArm Kuzmin, concentrated around Włodzimierz Wołyński. On 14 August Tukhachevsky had instructed Kuzmin to attack Hrubieszów and push on into the rear of any Polish force that might be assembling for an attack on his left flank. And although one of Kuzmin's divisions, Golikov's, did manage to take Hrubieszów, it got no further.[9]

By the time the Konarmia reached Sokal, the armies of the Western Front were in full retreat, and Tukhachevsky recognized that his orders were now pointless. 'The need for the Konarmia in the north had, to a certain extent, passed,' he lamely admitted, yet he was still considering throwing it into the fray on the grounds that 'every penny counts'. As he wavered on this point, the usually cautious Kamenev intervened, insisting that the raid on Lublin must go through as planned. The raid would, according to him, provide a 'useful diversion'.[10]

Accordingly, on 25 August Budionny, who still knew nothing of what had happened on the Vistula, set out from Sokal in support of a force whose remains were by then either in Polish captivity, being interned in East Prussia or slinking across the river Niemen in disorderly groups. He was charging into a battle that had already been fought and lost. To make matters worse, as he launched his raid into what was supposed to be the rear of a strike force that was already some four hundred kilometres away, another was gathering, bent on his destruction.

Once Gai's Konkorpus had slipped through his clutches, Sikorski, whose Fifth Army had become redundant, was sent south to take command of the Third Army on the Bug. The 9th Division from his Fifth Army and Żeligowski's 10th were to follow, and with this reinforced Third Army he was to lead an offensive into Volhynia and liquidate the Konarmia.

Budionny got off to a slow start. The physical exhaustion and draining morale of his men slowed the pace and robbed the Konarmia of its dash. After crossing the Bug and brushing aside units of the 2nd Legionary Division, the southernmost of the Third Army, it pressed on towards Zamość. But it was marching into a trap: the 2nd Legionary Division had merely wheeled round, taking up new positions along the Konarmia's right flank, while General Stanisław Haller's* 13th Division from the Sixth Army moved up from the south, threatening its left. By the time the Konarmia's leading units had reached Zamość, it was effectively

---

* Younger brother of Józef Haller, commander of the Blue Army and of the Northern Front during the battle of Warsaw.

caught in a long corridor between two Polish forces. That should not in itself have presented a problem, since Golikov and the rest of Kuzmin's army were moving up in support, and would prevent either of them from closing in.

On 29 August Budionny's 11th Division surrounded Zamość while the 6th Chongar bypassed it and moved on towards Lublin. But Zamość, an ancient fortress, was held by one of Żeligowski's regiments, which would be difficult to dislodge. And in its move on Lublin the Chongar Division had come up against the rest of Żeligowski's forces, raising the possibility that it might be caught between two fires. By the afternoon, Budionny was beginning to feel uneasy. His flanks were being hemmed in by two Polish infantry divisions, and Żeligowski was barring the road ahead.

That evening Budionny learned, from prisoners taken near Zamość, that Tukhachevsky had been routed on the Vistula and had fled back across the Niemen. The news, which came like a bolt from the blue, reduced the operation he was engaged on to complete nonsense. He was effectively invading Poland on his own, with 11,597 sabres, 1,418 bayonets, 387 machine guns and seventy-two field guns.[11]

By the next morning, the Konarmia was trapped in a narrow salient. Polish shells fired from both sides met in the middle. Budionny's original headquarters at Stara Antoniówka were demolished by Haller's artillery, his second, at Miączyn, were shelled by the 2nd Legionary, and he was eventually obliged to make do with a command post in a wood. Two days of torrential rain had turned the dusty roads into morasses. The Konarmia's artillery was finding it difficult to deploy. Its armoured cars were out of action. Horses slithered about and carts sank up to their axles in the mud. Even the *tachankas* were running into trouble and began jettisoning cases of ammunition. Budionny's car stuck in the mud, and he took to the saddle.

He spent most of that day, 30 August, riding back and forth inside the tightening ring with Voroshilov in search of a point at which to break out. News reached him that Polish cavalry had been sighted on the road from Tyszowce to Komarów. 'That was the alarm signal,' he writes, 'the enemy had moved into our rear.' He regrouped his forces so as to face Rómmel with his best units, the 4th and 6th Chongar, to which he added the Independent Brigade, a small but reliable unit composed of Bolsheviks.[12]

Meanwhile, Sikorski had arrived to take command of the Third Army. He quickly grasped that the situation was little short of ideal, with the Konarmia almost surrounded, but he also realized that this had occurred almost by chance, and that there was still no real communication between the various units closing in on the Russians.

Budionny had only two possible routes of escape: either the way he had come, through Tyszowce and Komarów, or through Werbkowice to Hrubieszów. Both were relatively narrow defiles through areas of marshland and low-lying terrain rendered impassable by the recent rainfall. Sikorski realized he would have to close off these exits before he put any more pressure on other sectors. Such a degree of coordination was not going to be easy to achieve: while the 2nd Legionary and the 10th Divisions were under his direct orders, Haller's 13th and Rómmel's Cavalry Division belonged to the Sixth Army.[13]

The next morning at dawn, Haller's 13th Division set off in a northerly direction from Komarów. It advanced in two columns, one of which was to strike northwards into the Konarmia's flank while the other made for Zamość to relieve the garrison. Rómmel was to move up in support of the first of these columns and shut off Budionny's line of retreat along the Komarów–Tyszowce road by occupying the Cześniki area. This was to be the scene of an epic struggle of a kind not witnessed in Europe for over a

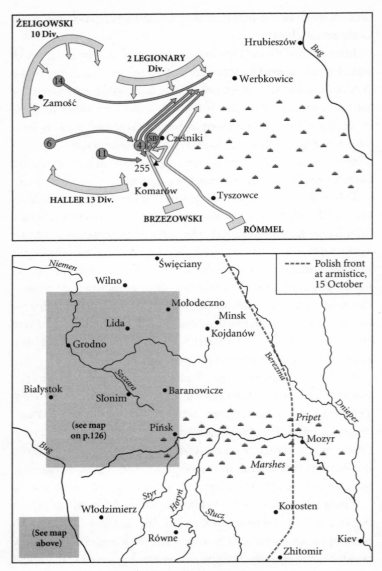

Budionny's last battle

century, and the last major cavalry-to-cavalry engagement in the Continent's history.

Rómmel had divided his force in two. The nearest to Cześniki was a brigade under Colonel Henryk Brzezowski, consisting of the 2nd Light Horse, the 8th Prince Józef Poniatowski Lancers and the 9th Galician Lancers, some 930 sabres and thirty machine guns in all. Brzezowski duly moved forward into the prescribed area, where he rapidly realized that a rise halfway between Komarów and Cześniki, marked '255' on the map, was the key. He therefore despatched the 2nd Light Horse to occupy it.

Before long, two thick columns of Red cavalry appeared from the north. One, Budionny's 11th Division, engaged Haller's infantry, to Brzezowski's left. The other, which turned out to be Timoshenko's 4th Division, bore down on Hill 255 and dislodged the light horsemen. Brzezowski stabilized the situation by throwing the 8th Lancers into the fray, but the two regiments were soon swamped by the superior numbers of the Cossacks, and he had to commit his last regiment, the 9th Lancers, which mounted a fine charge that drove them back to Cześniki. There it was brought to a halt by the appearance of a fresh brigade of Cossacks.

The horsemen of both sides deployed facing each other, and the commanders rode out of the ranks into the open space between. They drew their revolvers and twelve shots rang out in rapid succession. Neither fell. As the two duellists glared at one another in silence, a trooper galloped out of the Polish ranks and cut down the Russian with a slash of his sabre. This provoked a charge by the Cossacks, which drove the Poles back on to Hill 255.[14]

There followed a protracted mêlée, with the horsemen locked in hand-to-hand combat, hacking with their sabres, lunging with their lances and occasionally using their revolvers. The Poles only avoided being entirely swamped by remaining in tight formation, at squadron or even platoon level, tearing themselves away from the enemy in order to draw back and then charge. 'Every time a squadron was thrown back,' in the words of one participant, 'it would halt, about turn, and then charge once more with renewed impetus.' The action gave the impression of being fought in silence, as all that could be heard was the stamp of horses' hooves, the clink of tack, the sound of sabres clashing and the scuffling sound produced by the men, punctuated by the occasional word of command, bugle call, dying scream, gunshot or 'Hurrah!' of a unit trying to maximize the effect of a charge.[15]

This kind of fighting was physically exhausting, and could not be sustained. When he saw Budionny's 11th Division wheeling round on his left flank and his Independent Brigade taking up positions on his right, Brzezowski pulled all his men back and drew them up into a square, behind the machine guns. He was expecting Rómmel to come up with the other half of the Polish cavalry division, and he did not have to wait long.

As the Konarmia's Independent Brigade began to move against Brzezowski's flank it was caught side-on by a cavalry charge from the first of Rómmel's regiments, the 12th Podolian Lancers, led by Captain Tadeusz Komorowski.* The Independent Brigade beat a hasty retreat, and when Rómmel's other two regiments joined the action, supported by the division's artillery, so did the 11th and the 4th Divisions. The Polish lancers swept the field of battle and reoccupied Hill 255, closing the Konarmia's possible line of retreat through Komarów and Tyszowce. The cost had been high, with Brzezowski's brigade losing one-third of its effectives.

The trap was closing around Budionny. Żeligowski's 10th Division had reached Zamość and joined up with Haller's 13th. To the north, the 2nd Legionary Division was moving on Werbkowice,

---

* In the Second World War, as General 'Bór', Komorowski would command the Polish Home Army and lead it during the Warsaw Uprising of 1944.

where it was to link up with Rómmel. But Rómmel could not effectively seal the Werbkowice exit until he could persuade Haller to release Brzezowski's brigade by occupying Hill 255 with some of his infantry. Haller's response to his requests was sluggish.[16]

As he began to move north from Hill 255 shortly after midday, Rómmel was on the horns of a dilemma. He knew that three of Budionny's divisions were making a dash for Werbkowice, and he meant to thwart this. But he also knew that Budionny's fourth division, the 6th Chongar, was far behind them and some way south. If Rómmel were to take his whole force and march north on Werbkowice, the Chongar could not only slip through Komarów and out of the encirclement, they could take his own division in the rear and destroy it as it tried to block the way of the others. His orders were to make for Werbkowice, which he did, leaving Brzezowski on Hill 255 with instructions to follow on when his men and horses had recovered their strength from the morning's engagement.

Rómmel's chief-of staff, Captain Aleksander Pragłowski, took matters into his own hands and did not deliver to Brzezowski the order to follow on until 5.30 that afternoon. It was a nice piece of timing. Almost exactly an hour before, Budionny had ordered Pavlichenko, commander of the 6th Chongar, to attack the Poles on Hill 255 and then threaten Rómmel's rear in order to open the road through Werbkowice.

Shortly before 6 p.m., Brzezowski's men formed up into a column and began to move off, leading their horses by the reins. About a kilometre away, in the woods to the south of Cześniki, Budionny, still cutting a dash with his gaudy, silver-embroidered baggy red breeches, and an increasingly nervous Voroshilov, Mauser in hand, were doing their best to rouse the disheartened Cossacks of Pavlichenko's 6th Chongar Division for a final effort to destroy the Poles on Hill 255. 'To Warsaw!' shouted Voroshilov.

'Soldiers and commanders, in Moscow, our ancient capital, an unprecedented new power has been born. The first Government of Workers and Peasants orders you, soldiers and commanders, to attack the enemy and bring victory.' Then Pavlichenko, wearing a torn red tunic and brandishing a jewelled oriental weapon, ordered his men to draw sabres and led them into the charge.[17]

Captain Pragłowski was riding ahead of the Polish column, on his way to rejoin Rómmel. 'When I rode up the next rise,' he writes, 'I looked round and...froze. What I saw both fascinated and horrified me. At a distance of perhaps seven hundred metres dark waves of Cossacks were pouring out of the woods one after the other...' Another officer watching the same scene recalls that the mass of men emerged from the woods 'with a dull murmur, gradually turning into a blood-curdling howl as it drew closer'. 'The flood came closer and closer,' he writes. 'Curved sabres flashed in the last rays of the setting sun, red banners flapped, and chilling shouts and savage howls rent the air.'[18]

The 9th Lancers, who were marching at the tail of the column, mounted and deployed for a charge. The 8th, which was at the head of the column, followed suit a few minutes later. The gunners unlimbered where they stood and opened up on the approaching mass of Cossacks. The 9th Lancers, down to two hundred men after the morning's fighting, advanced slowly, sparing their horses, only breaking into a gallop at the last moment, and as they were in loose order they were almost immediately swamped. They began to give ground, then broke and fled, pursued by the Cossacks. The 8th Lancers were by this time trotting up in support, neatly drawn up in serried ranks which only parted for a moment to let the fleeing remnants of the 9th filter through. Then they charged.

The Cossacks had not seen this second regiment coming up in support, and were caught off guard. They came to a standstill, and when the wave of lancers collided with the hesitant front ranks, these gave way, precipitating the rest into flight. Within minutes, the Cossacks were diving back into the woods; only their *tachankas* saved them from further pursuit.

That night, the 6th Chongar Division joined up with the rest of the Konarmia, and on the following morning this forced its way out of the encirclement at Werbkowice. Budionny moved faster than the pursuing Poles, and on 2 September crossed the Bug, having made contact with Kuzmin's XII Army at Hrubieszów. He was safe once more. But the whole episode had been, in Babel's words, 'the beginning of the end for the 1st Cavalry Army'.[19]

Meanwhile, Tukhachevsky had managed to convince the baffled members of the Politburo that as a result of his 'tactical withdrawal' the situation was once more under control. Accordingly, on 2 September the Supreme Revolutionary War Soviet ordered Kamenev to reinforce the Western Front and pursue the campaign. Irritated by reports in the foreign press of the Soviet disaster, Chicherin sent a telegram, which was published in the London *Times* on 9 September. 'Polish and French wireless spreads false news about Polish victories. In reality, Russian forces are intact, retreat was executed in full order. Polish radios about a great victory are a fable.'[20]

Tukhachevsky and his comrades were determined to vindicate themselves, and over the next weeks worked with extraordinary energy at building up a new army. The disastrous situation of the Western Front on 25 August was mitigated by some favourable factors. The first was that, unlike Tukhachevsky's offensive, which had allowed the Poles no respite, Piłsudski's reached its logical term at the East Prussian border, and those Russian units that had managed to sidestep it and withdraw behind the Niemen were safe for at least a couple of weeks, the minimum time the Poles would require to regroup. The second was that, by falling back on his bases, Tukhachevsky now benefited from all the resources he needed. The quantities of men and equipment at his disposal were considerable. At Vitebsk, for instance, there were 70,000 uniformed and armed men ready to make good the losses of his mangled divisions.

There were also fresh formations available, and in the space of a week the Western Front acquired four new divisions – the 48th, 55th, Special Petrograd and 1st Cavalry – with the result that by 1 September Tukhachevsky reported that he could muster 85,097 men. This was remarkable, since only five days earlier the figure could have stood at little more than 30,000. He expected to have no fewer than 240,000 bayonets within three weeks.[21]

He redeployed Lazarevich's III Army, now his northern wing, along the Niemen around Grodno. It had survived the disaster better than the others, and after an infusion of 450 Bolsheviks from Petrograd and several thousand reinforcements it was ready for action. Next in line along the Niemen he stationed Kork's XV Army, which was awarded 1,000 Bolsheviks. Kork was also given Sollohub's two best divisions in exchange for the battered 33rd Kuban, which was withdrawn to Lida for reorganization. Sollohub's XVI Army was brought up to strength by the incorporation of two new divisions. Next in line was the IV Army, recreated by Tukhachevsky for the sake of appearances – the only thing this one had in common with its predecessor was Shuvayev himself.

Tukhachevsky assumed that the Poles would dedicate their main forces to dealing with the threat to Lwów and the Konarmia before regrouping to face him, by which time he must be in a position to launch a new offensive. 'We had every possibility of tilting the balance back in our favour,' he later wrote, 'but if the enemy were to attack before us, there was no doubt that we should be beaten. The whole problem amounted simply to which side would be ready to attack first.' But his calculations were incorrect.[22]

Piłsudski did indeed send five divisions south to help Sikorski deal with the Konarmia and clear the Bolsheviks out of Volhynia and Podolia. But he did not take his eye off Tukhachevsky, and while the five divisions of his strike force were resting along the East Prussian border he was sending every available unit from Warsaw to the Niemen. By 1 September they were taking up positions facing Tukhachevsky's forces. And while Sikorski was driving the Russian South-Western Front back to the river Horyń, nearly trapping Budionny for a second time in Równe, Piłsudski prepared his plan of action on the Niemen.

A few weeks earlier, when Tukhachevsky's armies had been closing in on Warsaw, the Soviets had signed an alliance with the Republic of Lithuania, buying the Lithuanians' friendship with the gift of Wilno and surrounding areas, which they had taken from Poland. But as this border was not recognized by Poland, Tukhachevsky's front was, in effect, anchored to nothing at its northern extremity.

Piłsudski's plan was to tie down Tukhachevsky's main forces around Grodno with a strong frontal assault, accompanied by diversionary attacks on Wołkowysk and Pińsk, while a mixed force of cavalry and infantry swept into the area held by the Lithuanians, avoiding engagements with them if possible, crossed the Niemen to the north and swung round in a deep arc into the Russian rear at Lida.

The attack, which began on 21 September, took Tukhachevsky by surprise. He nevertheless remained confident, as he had at least 120,000 men (his own calculation of 160,000 is probably too high) in strong positions with which to hold back the 90–100,000 Poles facing him. Lazarevich put up such a fight around Grodno that the Polish attack came to a standstill, and a fierce battle of attrition developed as Tukhachevsky committed more and more reserves to what he saw as a crucial contest: if his front cracked now it would

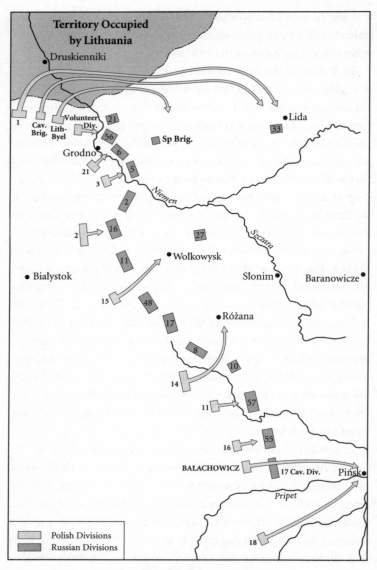

Territory Occupied by Lithuania

Druskienniki

1 Cav. Brig. Lith-Byel Volunteer Div. 21 56 6 5 Sp Brig. 33 Lida

Grodno

21 3 2 Niemen Szczara

2 16 27

11 Wołkowysk Słonim Baranowicze

Białystok

15 48 17 Różana

8 10

14

11 57

16 55

BAŁACHOWICZ 17 Cav. Div. Pińsk

Pripet

18

Polish Divisions
Russian Divisions

Last stand on the Niemen

give the lie to all his optimistic reassurances about a temporary setback, and would break what was left of the Red Army's morale. After three days' fighting, he had no reserves left.[23]

To Piłsudski the firm Russian stand was as baffling as it was worrying. His troops had taken prisoners from over a dozen different divisions in the fighting around Grodno, suggesting the presence of a huge force. He was not to know that in the chaos attendant on the rapid reorganization of the Russian armies men had been left with the markings and documents of their old units, or believed they still belonged to units which had ceased to exist. On the evening of 23 September he decided to bring one of the spearheads of the flanking force, the Lithuanian-Byelorussian Division, round in a shallower arc in order to threaten the Russians from the rear.[24]

Two days later, 25 September, the defence of Grodno began to slacken. Piłsudski ordered a general advance, and that evening the 21st Highland and the Volunteer Divisions fought their way into the city, while further south the 15th took Wołkowysk. Kamenev had that day ordered Tukhachevsky to pull back to Lida and the line of the river Szczara. But his order had been overtaken by events as the Russian armies began a retreat that in many cases turned into disorganized flight. Lazarevich, whose III Army was attempting a fighting withdrawal, soon found his road blocked by the Lithuanian-Byelorussian Division, and while his units broke through by sheer weight of numbers, they lost their will to fight, and communications between them broke down in the scramble for safety.

The retreat was more seemly in the centre of Tukhachevsky's line, largely thanks to Putna and his Siberians. He acted as the rearguard at the juncture of Kork's and Sollohub's armies, and frustrated Polish attempts to prise them apart. The picture was different further south along the line.

Krajowski's 18th Division, with General Bułak-Bałachowicz's Army of Byelorussia in the van, slipped past the left wing of

Shuvayev's IV Army. On 26 September, it emerged from the misty marshes to the north of Pińsk, Shuvayev's headquarters. Shuvayev took to his horse and rode west, to the safety of his front line, while most of his staff boarded a train and steamed off in the opposite direction. The IV Army disintegrated. Shuvayev's 17th Cavalry Division defected and joined Bałachowicz, and his other divisions retreated to the prescribed new line along the Szczara, but failed to stop on reaching it.

In the north, things were going from bad to worse for the Russians as the main spearhead of the Polish flanking force overpowered the 33rd Kuban Division, recuperating at Lida. When Lazarevich's retreating 21st reached the town, it surrendered to the Poles after a desultory fight. The other three divisions of Lazarevich's III Army were cut off. Some of their units tried to fight their way through, but most surrendered or dispersed, with the men retreating cross-country, singly or in small groups. In the centre, Kork and Sollohub were in full retreat.

Tukhachevsky was being bombarded from above with orders to hold on as long as possible: the peace negotiations begun at the instigation of the Entente were by now coming to a head, and it was imperative that the Russian armies be in possession of as much territory as possible before an armistice was agreed. When Kamenev protested that the only available reserves had no arms or even uniforms, Lenin retorted: 'I don't care if they have to fight in their underpants, but fight they must!' It was a race against time, as both sides grabbed at bargaining counters.[25]

On 28 September Tukhachevsky ordered a retreat to the line of Russian First World War trenches facing those in which the Poles had tried to make a stand back in July, and by 1 October his four armies had taken up positions in them. But the next day some of Kork's and Sollohub's units abandoned them to the advancing Poles. Like a wall that has not had time to harden, every

Russian position crumbled at the first push. Kamenev begged Tukhachevsky to brace his front and hold his positions for another week, but Tukhachevsky's political officer, Ivan Smilga, informed him that 'the divisions have completely lost the will and ability to fight'. According to Putna, a mood of defeatism had settled over their commanders as well.[26]

The Poles were determined to take back as much territory as possible before the impending ceasefire. On 9 October, Żeligowski took Wilno from the Lithuanians. The following day the 1st Legionary Division took Święciany. Kojdanów and Mołodeczno were occupied two days later. In the south, Rómmel's cavalry rode into Korosten on the tail of the retreating XII Army. On 15 October, the Poles captured Minsk and reached the Berezina.

The Polish armies were more or less where they had been in the spring, but now they were racing ahead virtually unopposed. What was left of the two armies of Lazarevich and Kork had been reduced to a retreating rabble, while Sollohub's and Shuvayev's had dwindled to skeleton forces. The road to Smolensk and Moscow lay wide open before Piłsudski's armies. South of the Pripet, the XII and XIV Armies of Kuzmin and Uborevich could no longer muster the strength of a full division between them, and did not attempt to hamper the Polish advance. The Konarmia had been withdrawn entirely. The men had begun deserting in large numbers, while those who remained took out their disappointment on the inhabitants of the villages and towns they passed through, particularly the Jews.

Even the seemingly limitless supply of manpower could not make up for the Russian losses which, counting dead, wounded, captured and interned, had by now passed the 200,000 mark. And that did not include the deserters, who would have accounted for a good few tens of thousands more. There was only one reserve the Soviet Republic could call on in the whole of western Russia, the VI

Army on the Latvian border, and this was duly sent to shore up the crumbling Western Front. But it would require more than a little reorganization to stabilize the situation.

The military débâcle had encouraged unrest all over Byelorussia and Ukraine. As the fourth winter since the Revolution drew near, there was no hint of improved conditions for anyone, and the authority of the Soviet Republic was being challenged. The garrisons of Smolensk and Viazma tottered on the brink of mutiny. Tens of thousands of deserters from the Red Army took to the forests, to join 'Green' bands in which they could at least ensure survival through looting.

Petlura was once more making for Kiev, with 30,000 men. Bałachowicz was taking possession of Byelorussia at the head of some 18,000 of his own, and a further 10,000 White Russians under General Peremikin and 2,000 Cossacks under Vadim Yakovlev were on their way to link up with the White Army of General Wrangel, which was advancing from the Crimea. The Bolshevik leadership faced one of its worst crises to date.

The only thing that could save it was a ceasefire. That came into effect on 16 October, and the Polish armies came to a halt. The VI Army, on its way from the Latvian border, did not even detrain at Smolensk; it trundled on southwards, to be used against Wrangel's Whites.

6

The Aftermath

Peace was finally signed between Poland and Russia at Riga on 18 March 1921. The Polish negotiators, eager to repair Poland's damaged image abroad, did not insist on her historic frontiers and settled for a compromise that nevertheless included much of Byelorussia and Ukraine within her borders. Nor did they attempt to accommodate an independent Ukraine in the settlement. Petlura was soon overwhelmed by the Red Army, and the remnants of his forces were disarmed as they sought refuge in Poland once more.

They, along with defeated White Russians and other oppressed minorities, regarded the peace, as did many outraged Poles and the Bolsheviks themselves, as no more than a truce in an ongoing struggle. And so it turned out to be. In 1939 the Soviet Union would seize the opportunity offered by Hitler to help itself to Polish territory up to a line roughly following that suggested by Lord Curzon in the summer of 1920. Two years later, many Petlurists, White Russians, Georgians and others would throw in their lot with Germany in the hope of ousting the Bolsheviks or gaining independence. In 1945 Stalin would achieve much of what he and Lenin had set out to do in 1920, but after 1989 it would be the turn of the heirs of Piłsudski and Petlura to triumph.

Seen in this context, the events of 1920 seem not only irrelevant, but almost quaint. The horrific Armageddon that rolled back and forth across the area two decades later, and the dark night of communism that engulfed it for half a century after that, make them appear almost Lilliputian. The frontiers which were deemed so important then were swept into oblivion. So were the state structures to which so much value had been attached. And so were a staggering proportion of the principal actors.

The officer who led the 8th Lancers into the charge at Komarów lived out his last years in West London under the premiership of Margaret Thatcher. Budionny had died in his bed a decade earlier at the grand old age of ninety-four, a hero of the Soviet Union. They were among the lucky ones.

In 1926 Petlura, whom destitution had forced into the profession of cabaret artiste, was assassinated on the boulevard St Michel in Paris by a young Jew whose parents had been killed during a pogrom in Kiev. The Polish chief-of-staff Rozwadowski, who as military governor of Warsaw resisted Piłsudski's coup d'état of 1926, died two years later in suspicious circumstances. Piłsudski himself died in 1935, having achieved cult status: in 1945 Marshal Zhukov took time off from pursuing the retreating Germans to visit his grave in the royal mausoleum in Kraków's cathedral. Zhukov and his comrade Timoshenko were also fortunate.

Between 1935 and 1938, Tukhachevsky, Gai, Sollohub, Sergeyev, Lazarevich, Kork, Putna, Yakir, Primakov, Uborevich and countless other senior officers were murdered in Stalin's purges. Even the wives of Tukhachevsky and Uborevich were declared 'enemies of the people' and shot in 1941. A year earlier, in 1940, Trotsky had been tracked down in Mexico by an assassin sent by Stalin, and murdered with an ice-pick. When Russia went to war in 1939, the Red Army was led by old cronies such as Budionny and Voroshilov, with predictable results.

Śmigły-Rydz, who commanded the Polish army in 1939, died in Warsaw in 1941. Others, including Stanisław Haller, General Skierski, the commander of the Fourth Army in Piłsudski's strike force, and Plisowski, the dashing young colonel of the 14th Lancers, were among the 20,000 Polish officers who ended up in the mass graves of Katyn and other places of extermination. The venerable Krajowski and many more perished in Nazi concentration camps, while Sikorski lost his life when his plane crashed into the sea shortly after taking off from Gibraltar in 1943. It is as though a curse had been cast on them. And it is difficult to shake off entirely the suspicion that Stalin's behaviour towards the Poles in the 1940s was tinged with revenge for the humiliation of 1920.

It had indeed been one, and the Bolshevik leadership was profoundly affected by it. The events had revealed the frailty and limits of their power. They also suggested that the whole world was ranged against them, and that the masses in other countries could not be relied on to support them. This gave rise to a siege mentality, isolationism and the doctrine of 'communism in one country', expressed to the outside world in a sulky, defensive aggressiveness. Hurt pride is in evidence in the attitude of most of Russia's leaders to the rest of the world, beginning with Lenin.

The isolation in which Russia spent the 1920s and 1930s undoubtedly assisted Stalin in his seizure of power and his reign of terror, and it ultimately pushed her into the arms of the other regime born of humiliation and fired by a determination to overthrow the Versailles settlement – Nazi Germany. And when his troops marched into Poland in support of the Germans in 1939, Stalin showed that he had learnt the lessons of 1919–20. There would be no attempt to win the Poles over to communism; his previous experience had taught him that they were not amenable. So he set about extirpating not only nobles, priests and landowners, but also doctors, nurses and veterinary surgeons, and in general anyone who might show the slightest sign of independent thought or even curiosity – the scores of charges which entailed immediate arrest and deportation included possessing a stamp collection. Over 1,500,000 people were caught up in this fine net. Army officers, for whom Stalin felt a particular hatred, were murdered in the forest of Katyn and elsewhere, other ranks and civilians were despatched to the Gulag, where a majority died. After 1945 he would do his best to extend the same principles to the rest of Poland.

How differently things might have turned out in Russia had some kind of peace been negotiated back at the beginning of 1919, and the whole war avoided, it would be idle to speculate. It would be equally pointless, if fascinating, to try to extrapolate the consequences of a Russian victory at Warsaw in 1920: Poland and the Baltic states would have been turned into Soviet republics, followed almost certainly by Czechoslovakia, Hungary and Romania, and very probably Germany, and the rest of Europe would have been profoundly affected; whether this would have led to world revolution or an international crusade leading to the destruction of Soviet Russia is anybody's guess. But some of the consequences of the war are there for all to see.

The events of 1919–20 affected attitudes not only in Russia and Poland, but throughout the region and even the world. They confirmed the belief that Russia would always remain an imperialist power and a threat to her neighbours, whoever was at the helm. They buttressed the right-wing conviction that socialism would never be a benign force in politics. This encouraged a certain mistrust of democracy and led many to favour governments led by 'strong men', even at the cost of some personal liberty. Mussolini, Admiral Horthy, General Franco, Salazar and Hitler, not to mention other less obviously dictatorial leaders, were all direct beneficiaries. And even where there was no direct threat apparent, as in mature democracies such as Britain and the United States, fear of the 'red peril' exerted a powerful influence. Cardinal Achille Ratti's presence in Warsaw in 1920 meant that both during his later nunciature in Germany and his reign as Pope Pius XI, anti-communism would be one of the prime considerations in the formulation of Vatican policy.

One of the more noteworthy consequences of the events of 1919–20, also felt in varying degrees throughout the world, was that they helped transform the residual anti-Semitism of the majority of the inhabitants of Europe into a political factor, and injected a rich mix of nutrients into the budding fantasies about Jewish and Masonic plots to destroy Christian civilization. The fact that there were Jews in prominent positions in the Soviet apparatus, that the short-lived communist regime in Hungary had been led by a Jew, that there had been Jews in the PolRevKom, that many of the Jews living in Byelorussia, Ukraine and Poland had welcomed the Red Army, that many of the intellectuals in the West who had taken the side of Bolshevik Russia were Jews, ineluctably identified *all* Jews with communism, notwithstanding the large numbers of Jews who had fled before the approach of the Red Army, been massacred by it, or had fought against it. And for the same reasons, societies such as Poland were apt to regard the Jews as traitors to the nation – even though it was not clear why any Jew living somewhere that had suddenly become part of a new nation should feel any loyalty towards it, and notwithstanding that tens of thousands of Jews had fought bravely in the ranks of the Polish army. These attitudes and assumptions were to have a long life, in many countries, and would contribute not a little to the horrors of the subsequent decades. They also thrived in Soviet Russia, where the Jews were viewed at best as unreliable, and more commonly as agents of a worldwide capitalist or Trotskyite plot to bring down the Soviet regime.

The war of 1920 also clouded perceptions among the military all over the world, and the discussion that followed it was rich in erroneous assumptions and consequently even more erroneous deductions. Participants and observers were quick to explain, excuse and blame. Tukhachevsky blamed the disaster on lack of coordination between the fronts, and bad luck. Other Russian commanders pleaded inferiority of numbers and equipment, and only a few, such as Putna and Sergeyev, put it down to Tukhachevsky's inability to concentrate his forces at the right points, combined with the assumption that Russian Civil War conditions would obtain in Poland.

In the West, the main preoccupation was not so much with how the war had been won, but by whom. When he heard of the victory at Warsaw, Lloyd George sent a communiqué congratulating Lord D'Abernon and General Weygand. Lord D'Abernon congratulated Lloyd George and, for reasons which remain obscure, the Chief of the Imperial General Staff Sir Henry Wilson. President Millerand congratulated Weygand, and decorated him with the Grand Cordon of the Légion d'Honneur. Despite several formal and many verbal rebuttals on his part, he was widely regarded as the author of the plan that had brought victory. The Poles distributed their congratulations according to political affiliation, personal loyalty or religious outlook: to Piłsudski, Sikorski, Haller, Rozwadowski or the Virgin Mary.

Little effort was made to analyse the campaign or to learn anything from it. General Radcliffe, an eyewitness, dismissed it as 'an eighteenth-century war'. Coming as it did just after the Great War, with its static trenches, its armies of millions and its heavy concentration of firepower, this campaign could not but stand out for its mobility. Large bodies of cavalry had led the action by carrying out deep flanking raids, while tanks and planes had failed to make an impact. These points were picked up by redundant cavalrymen and traditionalists all over the world, who used them to argue that cavalry still had an essential role to play in modern warfare. Only a handful drew the conclusion that the warfare of the future would indeed be one of deep thrusts and pincer movements, but that these would be carried out by a new generation of mobile armour. Among them were two participants in the campaign, De Gaulle and Sikorski, whose published reflections were read with interest but laid aside.

Yet although the war of 1920 taught many people the wrong lessons, making the Poles too trustful of training and morale, and the Russians too reliant on vast numbers when it would be superior weapons that carried the day, it did temper some of the finest commanders of the Second World War. And it did contribute to Allied victory in a crucial way: the Polish Army's concentration on radio monitoring, which led to its interest, from the late 1920s, in the use the Germans were making of the 'Enigma' encoding machine, lies at the origins of Bletchley Park, where the German codes were comprehensively broken, allowing the Allies to read most of the German army, navy and air force's orders.

And even if the Polish victory was soon cancelled out by what happened after 1939, the two decades of freedom from communism it bought for East Central Europe provided much of that part of the Continent with its first taste of some kind of democratic and civilized existence. This was certainly not always an edifying experience, and many of the countries in the region followed the lead of Italy, Spain and Germany by adopting more or less dictatorial forms of government.

Poland itself resisted this tendency at first. But its parliamentary politics were so bedevilled by squabbling and factionalism, understandable after over a century of political repression, that disenchantment grew on all sides of the political spectrum. In 1926, exasperated by the antics of the parliamentarians, Piłsudski emerged from retirement and staged a coup which, while far from bloodless, was neither particularly violent nor drastic in its impact. The only formal change was that the constitution was amended to give the president greater powers. But Piłsudski and his supporters hovered in the background, defying anyone to challenge their authority. The parliamentary opposition's power to affect policy dwindled and more obvious opponents such as communists were locked up or repressed by other means. After Piłsudski's death in 1935 it was his faithful supporters, many of them former Legionary officers, who pulled the strings. As they increasingly invoked national solidarity to deal with every problem, be it economic or political, they fostered ill-feeling between the ethnic Poles and the various minorities, such as the Germans, the Ukrainians and particularly the Jews.

Yet, imperfect as it may appear to a modern observer, that brief experience of democracy would allow the peoples of an area stretching from present-day Estonia down to the Balkans to develop and expand the institutions and forms of civil society – more successfully than has been generally acknowledged: in welfare and social housing, in the emancipation of women, in public education and in many other areas they outstripped older democracies such as France and Britain, not to mention the United States. And it was this, ultimately, that allowed them to survive, defy and eventually overcome both fascism and communism. The democratic and civic instinct in that part of Europe today is largely the product of the two decades of freedom secured by Piłsudski and his armies on the Vistula in 1920.

SOURCES

Chapter 1: Old Scores and New Dawns

1. Komarnicki, Tytus, *The Rebirth of the Polish Republic*, London 1957, 604

2. Piłsudski, Józef, *Rok 1920* (with the text of *Pochód za Wisłę* by M.N. Tukhachevsky), London 1941, 165

3. D'Abernon, Edgar Vincent Viscount, *The Eighteenth Decisive Battle of the World*, London 1931, 39

4. Hoover, Herbert, *The Years of Adventure*, London 1952, 356

5. Bubnov, A.S., Kamenev, S.S., Tukhachevskii, M.N., Eideman, R.P., *Grazhdanskaia Voina, 1918–21*, Vol. III, Moscow 1930, 152; *Direktivy Glavnovo Komandovania Krasnoi Armii*, Moscow 1969, no. 133; Piłsudski (1941), 147; see also: Degras, Jane, *Soviet Documents on Foreign Policy*, Vol. I, Oxford 1951 & *The Communist International*, Vol. I, Oxford 1956; Hunczak, Taras, ed., *Ukraine and Poland in Documents, 1918–1922*, 2 vols, New York 1983; *Krasnaia Kniga. Sbornik Dokumentov o Russko-Polskikh Otnosheniakh 1918–1920*, Moscow 1920; Davies, Norman, *White Eagle, Red Star*, London 1972 & *The Genesis of the Polish-Soviet War*, in *European Studies Review*, 1975, n. 1; Dziewanowski, M.K., *Piłsudski – A European Federalist*, Stamford, 1969; Wandycz, P., *Soviet-Polish Relations 1917–1921*, Harvard 1969

6. Mikhutina, I.V., *Polsko-Sovetskaia Voina 1919–1920gg*, Moscow 1994, 57; Wandycz, P., *Polish–Soviet Peace Talks 1920*, in *Slavic Review*, September 1965; Denikin, A.I., *Kto Spas' Sovetskuiu vlast ot gibeli?*, Paris 1937; Nowak (1993); *Istoria Grazhdanskoi Voiny v SSSR*, Vols III–IV, Moscow 1957–59

7. Komarnicki, 510, 516; Davies, Norman, *Lloyd George and Poland, 1919–1920* in *Journal of Contemporary History*, 1971, no. 3; see also: Howard of Penrith, Lord, *Theatre of Life*, Vol. II, London 1936 & Page Arnot, R., *The Impact of the Russian Revolution in Britain*, London 1967

8. Mikhutina, 153, 173–5; *Polsko-Sovetskaia Voina 1919–1920 (Raniee nie opublikovannie dokumenty i materially)*, Moscow 1994, 40, 43, 47; Kutrzeba, T., *Wyprawa Kijowska*, Warsaw 1937, 45; Deutscher, Isaac, *The Prophet Armed*, Oxford 1970, 458; Yegorov, I.E., *Lvov-Varshava*, Moscow 1929, no. AKA-1534L22; Nowak, Andrzej, *Rok 1920: pierwszy plan ofensywy sowieckiej przeciw Polsce*, in *Niepodległość* Vol. 29, Warsaw 1997, 15–17; Carley, Michael Jabara, *The Politics of Anti-Bolshevism: The French Government and the Russo-Polish War, December 1919 to May 1920*, in *Historical Journal*, Vol. 19, 1976

Chapter 2: Playing Soldiers

1. Trotskii, L.D., *Kak Vooruzhalas Revolutsia*, Vol. II, Moscow 1924, 123–4; Erickson, J., *The Soviet High Command*, London 1962, 33; see also: Fedotoff-White, D., *The Growth of the Red Army*, Princeton 1944; Liddel-Hart, B.H., *The Soviet Army*, London 1956; Wildman, Allan K., *The End of the Russian Imperial Army*, 2 vols, Guildford 1988

2. Deutscher, 412, 415

3. Przybylski, A., *Wojna Polska 1918–1920 roku*, Warsaw 1930, 35; De Gaulle, Charles, *Lettres, Notes et Carnets*, Paris 1980, 27, 33; see also: Bagiński, H., *Wojsko Polskie na Wschodzie*, Warsaw 1921; Mitkiewicz, Leon, *W Wojsku Polskim 1917–1920*, London 1986; Dowbór-Muśnicki, J., *Moje Wspomnienia*, Poznań 1937; Kopański, S., *Moja Służba w Wojsku Polskim 1917–1939*, London 1965; Lepecki, M.B., *W Blaskach Wojny*, Warsaw 1926; Zając, J., *Dwie Wojny*, London 1964

4. Saryusz-Bielski, T., in *Dziewiątak*, no. 53, London 1957; Karpus, Z., *Wschodni sojusznicy Polski w wojnie 1920 roku*, Toruń 1999

5. Żebrowski, M., *Polska Broń Pancerna*, London 1971, 85ff; see also: Hercuń, P., *Rakiety nad Frontem*, Warsaw 1930; Tatarchenko, E., *Krasnaia Aviatsia na Zapfronte*, in *Revolutsia i Voina*, 1920, no. 1;

Karolevitz, R., and Fenn, R., *Flight of Eagles: The Story of the American Kosciuszko Squadron in the Polish–Russian War 1919–1920*, Sioux Falls 1974; Murray, K.M., *Wings over Poland*, New York 1932; Piwoszczuk, M., *Zarys Historii Wojnej Pierwszego Pułku Czołgów*, Warsaw 1935; Chocianowicz, W., *Dzieje 1go Pułku Artylerii Lekkiej Legionów Józefa Piłsudkiego*, London 1967; Frolov, I., *Snabzhenie Krasnoi Armii na Zapfronte*, in *Revolutsia i Voina*, 11–15, Moscow 1921
6. Fervaque, Pierre, *Le Chef de l'Armée Rouge*, Paris 1928, 36
7. Komarnicki, 304
8. Teslar, T., *Propaganda Boszewicka podczas Wojny Polsko-Rossyjskiej*, Warsaw 1938; Nowik, G., *Zanim złamano 'Enigmę'. Polski radiowy wywiad podczas wojny z Boszewicką Rosją 1918–1920*, Warsaw 2004, 393; Peploński, A., *Wywiad w wojnie polsko-bolszewickiej 1919–1920*, Warsaw 1999
9. Erickson, 97

Chapter 3: Grand Designs
1. Erickson, 86–7; Yegorov, 15
2. Dziewanowski, 206–95; Palij, M., *The Ukrainian-Polish Defensive Alliance 1919–1921*, Edmonton 1995; Stachiw, M., & Sztendera, J., *Western Ukraine at the Turning Point of Europe's History, 1918–1923*, 2 vols, New York 1969–71
3. Kakurin, N.E. & Melikov, V.A., *Voina s Byelopoliakami 1920*, Moscow 1925, 95, 96, 97; Savostianov, P., *Komandarm Uborevich*, Moscow 1966, 85; Allen, W.E.D., *The Ukraine*, Cambridge 1942, 309; *Polsko-Sovetskaia Voina 1919–1920* (1994), 67, 93–109; Mezheninov, S.A., *Nachalo Borby s Bielopoliakami na Ukrainie v 1920 godu*, Moscow 1925
4. Machalski, T., *Ostatnia Epopeja*, London 1969, 19, 41–2; Kukiel, M., *Moja wojaczka na Ukrainie: wiosna 1920*, Warsaw 1995; Piskor, T., *Działania Dywizji Kawalerii na Ukrainie*, Warsaw 1926; Rybak, J., *Pamiętniki*, Warsaw 1954; Kutrzeba (1937), 95, 101; Kakurin & Melikov, 96, 97, 98, 106, 438; Adiutantura Generalna Naczelnego Dowództwa (AGND), Piłsudski Institute, London, file 9, no. 4322; Kmicic-Skrzyński, L., *Jak*

Patrol 1-go Pułku Szwoleżerów zajął Kijów, in *Przegląd Kawalerii i Broni Pancernej*, 59, London 1970; Bubnov, 291

5. De Gaulle (1980), 96; Karpus, Z., *Jeńcy i internowani rosyscy i ukraińscy w Polsce w latach 1918–1924*, Toruń 1991

6. Krzeczunowicz, K., *Ostatnia Kampania Konna*, London 1971, 28; Machalski (1969), 62; Kakurin & Melikov, 96; Carton de Wiart, Adrian, *Happy Odyssey*, London 1950, 96; Insarov-Vaks, M., *Moi Dokumenty*, Leningrad, n.d., 117–18; Kukiel, M., *Dzieje Polski Porozbiorowe*, London 1961, 575

7. Lenin, V.I., *Against the Plague of Nations: An Address to Thinking People on the Polish Question*, Cleveland 1920; Suslov, P.V., *Politicheskoye Obespiechenie Sovietsko–Polskoi Kampanii 1920 goda*, Moscow 1930; Macfarlane, L.J., *Hands Off Russia: British Labour and the Russo–Polish War, 1920*, in *Past and Present*, Vol. 38, December 1967; Posey, John P., *Soviet Propaganda, Europe and the Russo–Polish War 1920*, in *Southern Quarterly*, Vol. 6, 1968; Deutscher, 459–60; *Dokumenty i Materiały do Stosunków Polsko-Radzieckich*, Vol. III, Warsaw 1963, no. 7; *New Statesman*, London, 8 May 1920; Degras (1956), 91

8. De Gaulle, Charles, *Carnet d'un Officier Français en Pologne*, in *La Revue de Paris*, November 1920, 50; *Dokumenty i Materiały*, no. 11; Deutscher, 460; Bubnov, 325

9. Koritskii, N., *Marshal Tukhachevskii*, Moscow 1965, 231; Fervaque, 66, 75; *Marshal Tukhachevskii. Vospominania Druziei i Soratnikov*, Moscow 1965; Todorskii, A.I., *Marshal Tukhachevskii*, Moscow 1964; Nikulin, L., *Tukhachevskii*, Moscow 1963

10. Fervaque, 24; Dana, E., *Les origins de Toukhachevsky*, in *Le Monde*, Paris, 19 September 1967; de Goys, Général, *Toukhachevsky Intime*, in *L'Illustration*, Paris 1937

11. Bubnov, 318, 364

12. Piłsudski, 173

13. Piłsudski, 31, 38, 40; Kakurin & Melikov, 46; Sergeiev, I.N., *Ot Dviny k Visle*, Moscow 1923, 25; Zaremba, P., *Dzieje 15go Pułku Ułanów Poznańskich*, London 1962, 95; Szeptycki, Stanisław, *Front Litewsko-Białoruski*, Kraków 1925, 25

14. Tansky, M., *Joukov – Le Maréchal d'Acier*, Paris 1956, 29; Erickson, 51

15. Tiulienev, I., *Piervaia Konnaia v Boikh za Sotsialisticheskuiu Rodinu*, Moscow 1938, 142; Kakurin & Melikov, 441; Dubinskii, I.V. & Shevchuk, N.M., *Chervone Kozatstvo*, Kiev 1961; Kluiev, L., *Iaia Konnaia Armia na Polskom Fronte w 1920 godu*, Leningrad 1925

16. Carton de Wiart, 103; Pragłowski, A., *Wspomnienia o Bitwie Kawalerijskiej pod Komarowem*, in *Przegląd Kawalerii i Broni Pancernej*, London 1970; Machalski (1969), 91–2

17. Kakurin & Melikov, 116, 145; Kamenev, S.S., *Voina s Bieloi Polshei*, in *Voiennyi Viestnikh*, 12, Moscow 1922

18. Fudakowski, J. *Ułańskie Wspomnienia 1920 roku*, in *Przegląd Kawalerii i Broni Pancernej*, nos. 61–2, London 1971

19. Gul, R., *Tukhachevskii – Krasnoi Marshal, Berlin*, n.d., 134; Kutrzeba (1937), 151; Kakurin & Melikov, 153; Shmerling, P., *Kotovskii*, Moscow 1937

20. *Direktivy*, nos 696, 689, 690, 693; Budionnyi, S.M., *Proidenny Put'*, Vol. II, Moscow 1965, 99, 125–6, 131, 134, 136–8; Kakurin & Melikov, 161–2; Listowski, Antoni, Ms Memoirs, Czartoryski Library, Kraków Vol. III, 298ff

21. AGND, file 8, Sosnkowski's report, 22 June 1920, 3960; Krzeczunowicz, 129; Szeptycki, 40

22. Piłsudski, 42ff; AGND file 8, no. 3970, file 9, nos. 4341, 4342, 4354

23. Airapetian, G.A., *Legendarnyi Gai*, Moscow 1965

24. Kakurin & Melikov, 196, 200; Putna, Vitovt, *K Visle i Obratno*, Moscow 1927, 31; AGND, file 8, no. 4153, pp.3, 3884, 3967; Szeptycki, 26; Suslov (1930), 72

25. Kakurin & Melikov, 201

26. *Direktivy*, no. 643

27. Kakurin & Melikov, 201; Szeptycki, 65ff; Sergeiev, 49, 122; Piłsudski, 188; Żeligowski, L., *Wojna 1920 roku*, Warsaw 1930, 47ff; *Dokumenty i Materiały*, 145

28. *Direktivy*, 609; *Polsko–Sovetskaia Voina*, 117–21, 130–4; Davies, Norman, *Sir M. Hankey and the Inter-Allied Mission to Poland*, in *Historical Journal*, 1972, no. 3

29. Żarkowski, P., *Polska sztuka wojenna w okresie Bitwy Warszawskiej*, Warsaw 2000, 20–1; Musialik, Z., *General Weygand and the Battle of the Vistula*, London 1987; Weygand, Maxime, *Bój o Warszawę*, Warsaw 1930 & *Mirages et Réalités*, Paris 1957

30. Budionnyi, 170; Kuzmin, N., *Krushenie Posledievo pokhoda Antanty*, Moscow 1958, 100–101; Broniewski, W., *Pamiętniki 1918–1922*, Warsaw 1987, 183

31. Babel, Isaac, *1920 Diary*, Yale 1990, 41, 73

32. Babel, Isaac, *Konarmia*, Letchworth 1965, 97

33. Budionnyi, 214, 229

34. Machalski (1969), 112–39; Piłsudski, 47; Budionnyi, 261, 281; Babel (1965), 65; see also: Arciszewski, F. A., *Ostróg-Dubno-Brody*, Warsaw 1923; Berbecki, Leon, *Pamiętniki*, Warsaw 1959; *Chongarskaia 6aia Kavaleriiskaia Divizia*, Gomel 1924; Dubinskii, I.V., *Primakov*, Moscow 1968; Primakov, V.A., *Reid Chervonykh Kozakov*, Moscow 1925

Chapter 4: The Miracle on the Vistula

1. De Gaulle (1920), 40; Knyt, A.(ed.), *Rok 1920. Wojna Polski z Rosją Bolszewicką*, Warsaw 2005, 19; Merezhkowsky, Dymitr, *Joseph Piłsudski*, London 1921; see also Pietrzykowski, S., *Odwrót*, Poznań 1926

2. Piłsudski, 97

3. AGND, file 9, nos. 2297 & 4221

4. AGND, file 9, no. 4297; also Rozwadowski Papers, Piłsudski Institute, London, file 1, no. 23

5. Żeligowski, 117

6. Tarczyński, M. (ed.), *Bitwa Warszawska: dokumenty operacyjne*, Vol. I, Warsaw 1995, no. 356, p. 234; Pietrzak, H., *Sześć lat Wojny*, Łódź 1936, 234

7. Piłsudski, 48; Haller, J., *Pamiętniki*, London 1964, 224; *New Statesman*, London, 31 July 1920

8. Wyszczelski, L., *Operacja Warszawska*, Warsaw 2005, 89–90; Mikhutina, 190; Nowak (1993), 84

9. Piłsudski, 181, 44

10. Piłsudski, 204; Putna, 37; Szczepański, J., *Wojna Polsko–Sowiecka 1920 roku na Ziemi Wyszkowskiej*, Wyszków 1993, 23

11. S. Frydberg, unpublished memoirs, Polish Library, London, 133; Piłsudski, 204–5; *Direktivy*, no. 646

12. Budionnyi, 170, 281; Kuzmin, 100–1; see also *Leningradskaia Kavaleriiskaia Divizia 4-ya*, n.p. 1928

13. Budionnyi, 282

14. Budionnyi, 287

15. Frydberg, 119, 128

16. Piłsudski, 202

17. Putna, 76

18. Arciszewski, F.A., *Cud nad Wisłą*, London 1942, 165

19. Piątkowski, H., *Krytyczny Rozbiór Bitwy Warszawskiej 1920 roku*, in *Bellona*, London 1957, 9; Rozwadowski Papers, file I, nos. 10, 11, 18, 21, 25, 26; also *Bitwa Warszawska*, Vol. I, part 1, no. 4, p.697; Vol. 2, book 1, no. 3, p.383, no. 6, p.386; Jeleński, K.A., *Wywiad z Generałem Weygand*, in *Kultura*, 6/68, Paris 1953

20. Piłsudski, 104, 116

21. Piłsudski, 119; Rozwadzowski papers, file 1, no. 27; Order no 8358/III; Jędrzejewicz, W., *Kronika Życia Józefa Piłsudskiego 1867–1935*, Vol. I, London 1986, 509; *Bitwa Warszawska*, Vol. I, 15–18; Latinik, F., *Bój o Warszawę*, Bydgoszcz, n.d.; see also Kukiel, M., *Rozbiór Operacji Warszawskiej z punktu widzenia Obrony*, in *Bellona*, Warsaw 1926

22. Piłsudski, 206

23. Piłsudski, 208; Kakurin & Melikov, 286

24. Kakurin & Melikov, 281–4; *Direktivy*, nos 647, 644

25. Yegorov, 61; Wyszczelski, 214, 203

26. Piłsudski, 213; Tarczyński, 20

27. D'Abernon, 37; Witos, Wincenty, *Moje Wspomnienia*, London 1973, Vol. II, 300; Wędziagolski, K., *Pamiętniki*, London 1972, 425; Haller, 220; Carton de Wiart, 107; Arciszewski (1942), 16

28. Piłsudski, 123; Witos, 315; Glabisz, K., *Wspomnienia sierpniowe*, in *Bellona*, IV, London 1955; see also Waligóra, B., *Bój na przedmieściu Warszawy w sierpniu 1920r*, Warsaw 1934

29. Latinik

30. Putna, 116

31. Haller, 227

32. Sikorski, Władysław, *Nad Wisłą i Wkrą*, London 1942, 14ff; *Bitwa Warszawska*, Vol. II, Book I, part 2, no. 346.; Kakurin & Melikov, 286, 485; Biegański, S., *Bitwa Warszawska 1920 roku*, in *Bellona* I, London 1956; Wyszczelski, 246–50; see also Kowalski, Z.G., *5 Armia w bitwie warszawskiej*, in *Biuletyn Wojskowej Służby Archiwalnej*, 1995, no. 18; Lisiewicz, M., *Wspomnienia Adiutanta*, in *Dziennik Żołnierza*, 1942, no. 45

33. Sikorski, 56–70, 87, 114–15; Rozwadowski papers, file I, no. 32; *Bitwa Warszawska* Vol. II, book 1, part 2, 349–52, 355–61; Wyszczelski, 265–7

34. Sikorski, 129ff; Piłsudski, 211

35. Witos, 298

36. Witos, 299

37. D'Abernon, 37; Wędziagolski, 430

38. Sikorski, 106, 138; Machalski (1969), 142–60; Radecki-Mikulicz, Col., *Tworzenie 115/25 Pułku Ułanów Wielkopolskich i jego udział w wojnie 1920 roku*, in *Przegląd Kawalerii i Broni Pancernej*, 36, London 1964

39. Grzymała-Siedlecki, A., *Cud Wisły*, Poznań 1936, 99

40. Putna, 134

41. Wyszczelski, 348

42. Sikorski, 147

43. Machalski, T., *Zagon na Ciechanów*, in *Przegląd Kawalerii i Broni Pancernej*, 28, London 1962

44. Sikorski, 154; Podhorski, Z., *Wspomnienia Dowódcy 203 Pułku Ułanów z walk o Ciechanów w 1920 roku*, in *Wojskowy Przegląd Historyczny*, 1996, no. 4

45. Witos, 305

46. Piłsudski, 211

47. Piłsudski, 125; Rozwadowski papers, file 1, no. 37; Biegański; Żarkowski, 73, 84

48. Piłsudski, 125ff; Kakurin & Melikov, 286

49. Piłsudski, 126–8

50. Putna, 152; see also Kakurin, N., *Na puti k Varshave*, in *Revolutsia I Voina*, 1921, no.4

51. De Gaulle (1920), 49–50

52. Kakurin & Melikov, 319, 316ff; *Direktivy*, no. 657; Piłsudski, 213; Wyszczelski, 357; Mikhutina, 192, 208; *Polsko–Sovietskaia Voina*, 176, 187; Poltorak, S., *Pobedonosnoie Porazhenie. Razmyshlenia o Sovetsko–Polskoi voine 1920 goda v kanun yey 75-letia*, St Petersburg 1994, 151

53. Żarkowski, 101; Piłsudski, 214; *Direktivy* no. 652; Kakurin & Melikov, 320

54. Putna, 167

55. Kakurin & Melikov, 322; Putna, 166; Lenin, V.I., *Voiennaia Perepiska*, Moscow 1956, 246; Wyszczelski, 374–5

56. Kakurin & Melikov, 322–3; Budionnyi, 318

57. *Direktivy*, no. 661; Pospelov, P.N., *Istoria Komunisticheskoi Partii Sovetskovo Soiuza*, Moscow 1968, Vol. III, 489

58. *Direktivy*, no. 653, p.660ff; Bubnov, 456

59. Piłsudski, 415; Borkiewicz, A., *Dzieje 1go Pułku Piechoty Legionów*, Warsaw 1929, 833; De Gaulle (1980), 98

60. Wyszczelski, 381–4; Żukowski, Stanisław, *Działania 3go Konnego Korpusu Gaja*, Warsaw n.d.

61. Sikorski, 205, 203–4, 209; Kakurin & Melikov, 341; Gai, G.D., *Otkhod III Konkorpusa na Zapfrontie*, in *Revolutsia i Voina*, 4–5, Moscow 1921 & *V Germanskom Lagre*, Moscow 1931; Wyszczelski, 453

62. Putna, 168–9, 181

63. Putna, 176, 242

Chapter 5: Settling the Scores

1. Sikorski, 249–50; Karpus, Z., *Problem internowanych*, 176; Karpus (1991), 50; Wyszczelski 491–3; Żarkowski, 160, 188; Kakurin & Melikov, 351, 510

2. Piłsudski, 217; Budionnyi, 225; on this subject, see also Triandafilov, V., *Vzaimodieistvie miezhdu Zapadnom a Iuzhno-Zapadnom Frontami*

vo vremia lietniavo nastuplenia Krasnoi Armii na Vislu v 1920 godu, in *Voina i Revolutsia*, II, Moscow 1925

3. Kakurin & Melikov, 248; Yegorov, 80; Piłsudski, 208; Budionnyi, 318

4. *Direktivy*, no. 654; Budionnyi, 294, 311

5. Budionnyi, 318, 321

6. Aleksander Pragłowski, interview, London 1973; for the ensuing events, see: Rómmel, J., *Moje Walki z Budiennym*, Lwów 1937 & *Kawaleria Polska w pościgu za Budiennym*, Lwów n.d.

7. Kakurin & Melikov, 346

8. Budionnyi, 340

9. Kakurin & Melikov, 345

10. Kakurin & Malikov, 347, 363

11. Budionnyi, 357ff.; Kakurin & Melikov, 511

12. Budionnyi, 360–7, 358, 269

13. Bołtuć, M., *Budionny pod Zamościem* in *Bellona* XXII, Warsaw 1926

14. Machalski (1969), 176–8; Wyszczelski, 486

15. Machalski (1969), 178; interviews with A. Pragłowski & Kornel Krzeczunowicz, London 1973

16. Budionnyi, 366; Kakurin & Melikov, 351; Pragłowski & Krzeczunowicz interviews

17. Pragłowski interview; Budionnyi, 364; Babel (1965), 134–7; Babel (1990), 89

18. Pragłowski (1970); Machalski (1969), 182

19. Babel (1990), 90

20. *Direktivy*, no. 664

21. Kakurin & Melikov, 365, 510, 363; Kutrzeba, T., *Bitwa nad Niemnem*, Warsaw 1926, 10

22. Piłsudski, 216

23. Kutrzeba, 42, 92, 99, 91; Putna, 215

24. Kutrzeba, 110

25. Lenin, 246

26. Kakurin & Melikov, 383, 397–9; Putna, 218

FURTHER READING IN ENGLISH

Political background

Carley, Michael Jabara, *The Politics of Anti-Bolshevism: The French Government and the Russo-Polish War, December 1919 to May 1920*, in *Historical Journal*, Vol. 19, 1976

Davies, Norman, *White Eagle, Red Star*, London 1972

— *Sir M. Hankey and the Inter-Allied Mission to Poland*, in *Historical Journal*, 1972, no. 3

— *Lloyd George and Poland, 1919–1920*, in *Journal of Contemporary History*, 1971, no. 3

— *The Genesis of the Polish–Soviet War*, in *European Studies Review*, 1975, no. 1

Degras, Jane, *The Communist International*, Vol. I, Oxford 1956

Fiddick, Thomas C., *The 'Miracle of the Vistula': Soviet Policy versus Red Army Strategy*, in *Journal of Modern History*, Vol. 45, 1973

— *Russia's Retreat from Poland, 1920: From Permanent Revolution to Peaceful Coexistence*, New York 1990

Komarnicki, Tytus, *The Rebirth of the Polish Republic*, London 1957

Lenin, V.I., *Against the Plague of Nations: An Address to Thinking People on the Polish Question*, Cleveland 1920

Macfarlane, L.J., *Hands Off Russia: British Labour and the Russo–Polish War, 1920*, in *Past and Present*, Vol. 38, December 1967

Page Arnot, R., *The Impact of the Russian Revolution in Britain*, London 1967

Palij, Michael, *The Ukrainian-Polish Defensive Alliance 1919–1921*, Edmonton 1995

Posey, John P., *Soviet Propaganda, Europe and the Russo–Polish War 1920*, in *Southern Quarterly*, Vol. 6, 1968

Stachiw, M., and Sztendera, J., *Western Ukraine at the Turning Point of Europe's History, 1918–1923*, 2 vols, New York 1969–71

Wandycz, Piotr S., *Soviet–Polish Relations, 1917–1921*, Harvard 1969

Żółtowski, Adam, *Border of Europe*, London 1950

Military studies

Cisek, Janusz, *Kościuszko, We are Here! American Pilots of the Kościuszko Squadron in Defense of Poland 1919–1921*, London 2002

Erickson, John, *The Soviet High Command*, London 1962

Fedotoff-White, D., *The Growth of the Red Army*, Princeton 1944

Kaden-Bandrowski, Juliusz, *The Great Battle on the Vistula*, trs. Harriet E. Kennedy, London 1921

Karolevitz, Robert F., and Ross S. Fenn, *Flight of Eagles: The Story of the American Kosciuszko Squadron in the Polish–Russian War 1919–1920*, Sioux Falls 1974

Liddel-Hart, B.H., *The Soviet Army*, London 1956

Murray, Kenneth Malcolm, *Wings Over Poland*, New York 1932

Musialik, Z., *General Weygand and the Battle of the Vistula*, London 1987

Piłsudski, Józef, *Year 1920*, New York 1972 (contains Tukhachevskii, M.N., *The March Beyond the Vistula*)

Wildman, Allan K., *The End of the Russian Imperial Army*, 2 vols, Guildford 1988

Biographies and Memoirs

Babel, Isaac, *Red Cavalry*, London 1929

— *1920 Diary*, Yale 1990

Budienny, S.M., *The Path of Valour*, Moscow 1972

D'Abernon, Edgar Vincent, Viscount, *The Eighteenth Decisive Battle of the World*, London 1931

Carton de Wiart, Adrian, *Happy Odyssey*, London 1950
Deutscher, Isaac, *The Prophet Armed*, Oxford 1970
Dziewanowski, M.K., *Piłsudski – A European Federalist*, Stamford 1969
Howard of Penrith, Lord, *Theatre of Life*, Vol. II, London 1936
Patterson, E.J., *Pilsudski, Marshal of Poland*, London 1936
Reddaway, W.F., *Marshal Pilsudski*, London 1939
Zamoyski, Adam, *Paderewski*, London 1982

INDEX